WHO HAS BEWITCHED YOU?

EVER ASCENDING:
THE RESURRECTION SERIES VOL. 2

L. Emerson Ferrell

Voice Of The Light Ministries

Voice Of The Light Ministries

WHO HAS BEWITCHED YOU? © 2015 L. Emerson Ferrell
EVER ASCENDING: THE RESURRECTION SERIES VOL. 2

All rights reserved. This publication may not be reproduced or transmitted in any form or any means, filed in an electronic system nor transmitted in any electronic, mechanical way including photocopying, recording or by any information storage retrieval system, or in any other manner (including audiobooks), without the previous written permission of the author.

All Scripture quotations, *unless indicated otherwise*, have been taken from the New King James Version (NKJV) © 1982 by Thomas Nelson Inc., used by permission. All rights reserved.

Category	Reformation
Published by	Voice of The Light Ministries P.O. Box 3418 Ponte Vedra, Florida 32004 www.voiceofthelight.com
Printed in	The United States of America
ISBN 10 ISBN 13	1-933163-42-9 978-1-933163-42-0

TABLE OF CONTENTS

	Introduction	5
1	Lasting Impressions	9
2	My Early Church Years	13
3	The Modern Day Galatia Church	25
4	Foundations	37
5	Word Of Faith	43
6	Have Faith In God	49
7	Faith Is In The Truth Of What Christ Did	59
8	The Spirit Of Prophecy Revealed	65
9	Resurrection Deception	71
10	The Prophetic Is Historically Proven	83
11	The Week That Changed The World	99
12	The Week That Fulfilled The Law	129
13	Wave Offering	139
	Conclusion	143

INTRODUCTION

The Lordship of Christ is known throughout the universe in both the visible and invisible dimensions. Therefore, in order for the defeated powers and principalities to control people, they use the spirit of witchcraft, which is most often facilitated by religion.

The definition of *bewitched* is enchantment or fascination. This was the same enemy Paul faced in Galatia and it is the same spirit the church is facing today. The major purpose of that spirit is to create doubt and unbelief making persons use their reason, which ultimately perverts the authority of Christ. The first step in that process is to convince the new believers that the foundation of the Bible is about Moses and The Law instead of Christ Jesus.

> *O foolish Galatians! Who has bewitched you that you should not obey the truth, before whose eyes Jesus Christ was clearly portrayed among you as crucified?*
>
> *Galatians 3:1*

Paul was rebuking the church in Galatia because they were following the Laws of Moses instead of following the Spirit of God through faith. The same thing is happening today and it begins by discounting the words of Jesus as a prophet, which in essence makes Him a liar.

There is nothing more important for a Christian to believe than what Jesus Christ accomplished through His death and resurrection. In fact, the power of Christianity over every other religion in the world is embodied in the reality of the cross of Christ. Moreover, His resurrection from the grave, after three days and nights in the heart of the earth, separates Christianity from every other religion on the face of the planet.

Therefore, the only way the enemy could neutralize or destroy the authority of Christianity over all other religious system in the world would be to corrupt the resurrection of Christ Jesus.

This is exactly what the enemy has achieved every Easter when millions of Christians around the world celebrate Good Friday and Resurrection Sunday, even after Jesus said plainly in Matthew:

> *But He answered them, "An evil and adulterous generation seeks after a sign, but no sign will be given it but the sign of Jonah the prophet.*
> *For as Jonah was three days and three nights in the belly of the whale, so will the Son of Man be three days and three nights in the heart of the earth."*
> *Matthew 12:38-39*

The only sign Jesus promised that would prove He is the Son of God is that He would remain in the earth three days and three nights. But tradition, doctrine and ignorance have prevailed to single handedly bewitch the church and corrupt the only proof Jesus said would prove His divinity.

The sad truth of the matter is, we, and I include myself in this indictment, have no right to call Jesus Lord if we celebrate the lie of a Friday crucifixion and Sunday resurrection.

It is the most abominable witchcraft ever to be perpetuated on the church. In fact, the reason for this book is to break the spell that has been cast over those who love Jesus and want to follow the resurrected Christ. I have repented for following the lie and have written this book to open the eyes of every believer who has the courage to call a lie a lie and refuse to blindly follow tradition any longer.

This book is not written to rebuke but to enlighten you to the truth. It is written to prepare you for the greatest adventure of your life, which is the freedom from religion and witchcraft. The Spirit of Truth will set you free in the same manner He did me.

Be assured that if you have the courage to discover the truth, the Bible will become the easiest manual for revelation you will ever read. There is nothing that can prevail in the light of God's truth.

Please understand that if this spirit of witchcraft can keep you blinded by making you believe it makes no difference when Jesus was crucified, he can systematically destroy every prophetic word ever spoken in the scriptures.

As an Example, everything written prophetically in Daniel and Revelation are dependent on the exact timing of what Jesus did as our Passover Lamb. I will show you in this book, and the ones to follow, the exact timing spoken to Daniel by Gabriel is tied to our Lord's death and resurrection.

Furthermore, and perhaps more importantly, the whole Bible itself is written about Christ, which means that every detail of His birth, death and resurrection would be chronologically correct and accurate to the very year, day and hour.

I challenge you to read this book with an open mind and then study the scriptures for yourself. If after you have finished this book you choose to follow your traditions and doctrines then so be it. At least you have been exposed to another point of view.

Chapter 1

Lasting Impressions

There are certain incidents in all of our lives that form a lasting impression. One such event happened to me when I was 12 years old that marked me forever.

We had just finished our nightly family dinner outside on our backyard picnic table. My parents were discussing family business and my brothers were arguing over whose turn it was to do the dishes.

I was thinking about the day when suddenly, up in the night sky I saw a streaking light pass from east to west in the blink of an eye. Immediately, I shouted at the top of my lungs, "Look, a falling star." Everyone stopped talking and looked quickly in the direction I was pointing. "Awe, you missed it," I said.

My younger brother looked at me and said, "Do you think it was a star or a spaceship?" That comment drew snickers from my other brother and a smile from my father who knowingly nodded his head and said, "The universe is a sea of infinite unknowns."

"Maybe it was an angel," I said. My Sunday school teacher has been teaching us that before Jesus returns angels will fill the skies preparing the church to be raptured. Furthermore, she said, the problems in the world are a sure sign we are living in the "end times."

"What is that?" my brothers asked the teacher. "You mean no one taught you about Armageddon or the return of Jesus?" she replied.

"Well, they handed out pictures and drew charts describing these horrific events they said the book of Revelation described." he said, and then added, "It looked like a science fiction movie."

My brother then turned and asked me if I believed their explanations? I said, "To me it was the most exciting stuff I had ever heard."

So, I began to describe the "end-time dispensational doctrines" according to the theologians who used the Scofield Bible as their commentary. This Bible was used to train the Evangelical church leaders during the 19th and 20th century, which is when the theory was constructed.

I will never forget the look on my brothers' faces when I began to tell them about the earth being destroyed by fire after the Christians are "raptured" in order for God to save His chosen people, the Jews. At that point my father stood up and pointed his finger at me and said, "Who do you think you are?"

"Son," he said, "It is never wise to speak with such conviction about things that you learn from others."

He went on to say, "Remember, a wise person will only speak about things he or she personally experiences."

My father was a man of few words but when he spoke all of us listened. He did not go to church often nor was he considered a religious person, but I do believe God spoke through him on a number of occasions. His rebuke to me about speaking on that subject was one of those times.

I have remembered those words from my father and it has helped me throughout my life. Moreover, his reprimand has driven me to experience the "living" Christ in such a way that my fears about the future have been replaced by the knowledge of His completion of His assignment for all mankind. It is my prayer that this book will provoke you to experience Him in a new fresh way as well.[1]

---

[1] *As a footnote and because this is not the main subject contained in this book, anyone unfamiliar with the terms, rapture, Scofield Bible, post or premillennial, end times or dispensationalist should search the Internet. There are many articles and books written on these subjects.*

CHAPTER 2

MY EARLY CHURCH YEARS

My first experience with Christ occurred while watching a *Billy Graham* Crusade on Television. The power and conviction of his faith in Christ Jesus was a magnet that drew countless thousands of people to experience salvation through God's Son.

I know, because I was one of those who experienced the reality of Jesus dying for me on the cross. I believe something tangibly happened to me that day that started a transformation in my soul.

Over the years, I have discovered that most people whose lives are changed describe some type of an encounter with Jesus on the cross. Those experiences are real and heart felt. They produce both an emotional and divine love for the sacrifice Jesus made for each man, woman and child.

The tangible encounter I felt watching Billy Graham caused me to weep like a baby and compelled me to both ask God to forgive my sins and accept me into heaven after I died. Later I learned the Holy Spirit was the "presence" I felt emanating from the television. Since that time I've experienced Him in many ways and forms.

Billy Graham's impact on my life, and countless thousands, is an eternal testimony to His genuine experience and relationship with The Spirit of God.

After my experience with God, our family joined and attended the largest Baptist church in our city. There, my brothers and I were taught the Bible according to the traditions and doctrines of the Southern Baptists. I remember being baptized the first time at the age of 13.

We attended that church until my mother decided she wanted to move to another church. It was never quite clear to us why she wanted to move. Later I learned her interpretation of the Bible differed from the pastor, to the extent that she wanted to go somewhere else. We left that church and joined a non-denominational church closer to our home.

Our family became very familiar with the most popular doctrines and beliefs of the mainstream "Christian Church."

The common denominator among all the churches we attended seemed to be salvation through the cross of Jesus and His future return. That was the central theme mixed with the constant teaching that Israel was God's chosen people. Strangely enough that remains the same theme today in most evangelical churches.

Attending all the various churches have prepared me in many ways and I do not regret any of those times. The Lord uses every step we make towards Him, knowingly or unknowingly, to reveal more of Himself. I am eternally grateful to my mother and father for taking me to church and providing me with an opportunity to pursue Christ.

The journey to know Christ does not depend on where you begin as long as you realize it never ends. It is very important to recognize that the initial encounter with Jesus Christ is only the beginning of greater and greater experiences with the living Word.

We all are inclined to associate events with surroundings. For example, if a baseball player hits a home run or a golfer has a hole-in-one, many of them will try to repeat that outcome by wearing the same clothes or eating the same foods before the next game or tournament. This is known as a superstitious behavior, which is defined by Webster's dictionary to mean, a belief or way of behaving that is based on fear of the unknown and faith in magic or luck: a belief that certain events or things will bring good or bad luck.

Most religious denominations and doctrines are formed after the founder has had an experience with the Spirit of God. These religious structures produce followers whose behavior becomes superstitious. God responds to faith not a doctrine or superstitious behavior.

Moreover, there is a tendency to connect a supernatural experience such as a healing or deliverance with the denomination or "church" where this encounter occurred, thereby forming a superstitious attachment to that particular doctrine or tradition.

Each and every encounter with the living Christ is a joyous one, but rest assured it is only the beginning of our adventure to know Him. It is absolutely critical to resist the urge to think we have "arrived" and that God approves of all the doctrines or messages of the denomination where we first encountered His presence.

As I look back at my experiences, in the various churches I attended, I'm reminded of my conviction that I too had "arrived" and God approved this denomination and doctrines.

Men who had supernatural encounters from the Holy Spirit formed most of our current day denominations. Nevertheless, instead of pursuing the invisible realm of the Spirit they built doctrines and theologies around those experiences.

This reminds me of the events on the mount of Transfiguration when Peter wanted to build a tabernacle for Jesus, Moses and Elijah and he was rebuked by God.

> *And He was transfigured before them. His face shone like the sun, and His clothes became as white as the light.*
>
> *And behold, Moses and Elijah appeared to them, talking with Him.*
>
> *Then Peter answered and said to Jesus, "Lord, it is good for us to be here; if You wish, let us make here three tabernacles: one for You, one for Moses, and one for Elijah."*
>
> *Matthew 17:2-4*

God used the Old Testament tabernacle model as the shadow of Christ who builds His church inside each believer, in order for the Holy Spirit to guide us into all truth.

Throughout the years, it has been made abundantly clear to me that God will use anything or anybody to introduce Himself to us. But at that point, He makes it our responsibility to continue the relationship with Him via our spiritual connection and resist the tendency to depend on a man or a system to train us.

Herein lies the problem with all the systems of religion. Regardless, of how good the intentions are in the beginning to worship God, eventually, over time, the man or the denomination becomes the center of attention instead of God.
The model to create a denomination has been used for centuries and starts by building a physical building and calling it a church. Moreover, because it requires a way to distinguish itself from other denominations they create laws or doctrines according to their interpretations of the scriptures.

It becomes a form without substance because it cannot reproduce spiritual beings but rather sheep that follow the doctrines of man.

God is Spirit and the only One who can train us is the Holy Spirit. The Spirit speaks directly to our spirit about the ways and wonders of our Father. It is through these interactions that we can develop a relationship with Him. This is the beginning of our endless journey to know Him.

> *Do you not know that you are a temple of God and that the Spirit of God dwells in you?*
>
> *1 Corinthians 3:16*

From the times of Moses to Jesus the physical "tabernacle" was the foreshadow of the future Temple built from the blood of Christ.

> *This served as the copy and shadow of the heavenly things, as Moses was divinely instructed when he was about to make the tabernacle. For God said to him, "See that you make all things according to the pattern shown you on the mountain."*
>
> *But now He has obtained a more excellent ministry, inasmuch as He is also Mediator of a better covenant, which was established on better promises.*
>
> *For if that first covenant had been faultless, then no place would have been sought for a second.*
>
> *Hebrews 8:7*

Before the foundation of the world God and His Word had prepared covenants for mankind. The first was temporary, in order to confound satan and manifest Christ. He accomplished both.

Jesus supplied what the first covenant could not with His blood and obedience. Man will never again need the sacrifice of animals to restore his relationship with God. Jesus finished the work and is seated at the right hand of His Father.

Just as the Old covenant was removed so was the need for a temple. We are the temple of God. Once we are born into Christ, we become both His Body and temple for His Spirit.

There is no doubt when God destroyed the Jerusalem Temple in 70 AD it was intended to be permanent. The article below both reinforces that and reminds us that our New Covenant is the greater of the two.

GOD DESTROYS THE TEMPLE IN 70 AD

Thus says the Lord: Heaven is My throne, and the earth is My footstool. What kind of house would you build for Me? And what kind can be My resting-place?

Isaiah 66:1 AMP

The following documents are historical evidence that God not only destroyed the temple, as prophesied by Jesus, but also would never allow it to be rebuilt.

Socrates of Constantinople also known as Socrates Scholasticus, a 5th-century Christian church historian, first, wrote this. He is the author of a Historia Ecclesiastica, "Church History," which covers the history of late ancient Christianity during the years 305–439.[2]

This account from The Ecclesiastical History Book III, Chapter XX, in A Select Library of Nicene and Post-Nicene Fathers of the Christian Church, Second

---

[2] *https://en.wikipedia.org/wiki/Socrates_of_Constantinople*

Series, II, contains the account of an attempt to rebuild of the Temple[3][4]:

"The emperor, the other pagans, and all the Jews, regarded every other undertaking as secondary in importance to this. Although the pagans were not well disposed towards the Jews, yet they assisted them in this enterprise, because they reckoned upon its ultimate success, and hoped by this means to falsify the prophecies of Christ. [Since Jesus in the New Testament had prophesied the destruction of the Temple, its rebuilding would make of him a false prophet.] Besides this motive, the Jews themselves [relying on the sympathy of Julian] were impelled by the consideration that the time had arrived for rebuilding their Temple."

"When they had removed the ruins of the former building, they dug up the ground and cleared away its foundation; it is said that on the following day when they were about to lay the first foundation, a great earthquake occurred, and by the violent agitation of the earth, stones were thrown up from the depths, by which those of the Jews who were engaged in the work were wounded, as likewise those who were merely looking on. The houses and public porticos, near the site of the Temple, in which they had diverted themselves, were suddenly thrown down; many were caught thereby, some perished immediately, others were found half dead and mutilated of hands or legs, others were injured in other parts of the body."

"When God caused the earthquake to cease, the workmen

---

[3] *Graetz, 111, pages 595-603*

[4] *Elbogen. pages 14-18; Roth, pages 140-148, Golub, J. S., Medieval Jewish History, Sec. I; Sec. III, "The Christian Church."*

who survived again returned to their task, partly because such was the edict of the emperor, and partly because they were themselves interested in the undertaking. Men often, in endeavoring to gratify their own passions, seek what is injurious to them, reject what would be truly advantageous, and are deluded by the idea that nothing is really useful except what is agreeable to them. When once led astray by this error, they are no longer able to act in a manner conducive to their own interests, or to take warning by the calamities, which are visited upon them."

"The Jews, I believe, were just in this state; for, instead of regarding this unexpected earthquake as a manifest indication that God was opposed to the re-erection of their Temple, they proceeded to recommence the work. But all parties relate that they had scarcely returned to the undertaking, when fire burst suddenly from the foundations of the Temple, and consumed several of the workmen."

"This fact is fearlessly stated, and believed by all; the only discrepancy in the narrative is that some maintain that flame burst from the interior of the Temple, as the workmen were striving to force an entrance, while others say that the fire proceeded - directly from the earth. In whichever way the phenomenon might have occurred, it is equally wonderful."

"A more tangible and still more extraordinary miracle ensued; suddenly the sign of the cross appeared spontaneously on the garments of the persons engaged in the undertaking. These crosses looked like stars, and appeared the work of art. Many were hence led to confess *that Christ is God, and that the rebuilding of the Temple was not pleasing to Him; others presented themselves in the church, were initiated, and besought Christ, with hymns and supplications, to pardon their transgression. If any one does not feel disposed to believe my narrative, let him go and be convinced by those who heard the facts I have related from the eyewitnesses of them, for they are still alive."*

"Let him inquire, also, of the Jews and pagans who left the work in an incomplete state, or who, to speak more accurately, were unable to commence it."[5]

This is exactly what Jesus prophesied:

... And said, "This fellow said, 'I am able to destroy the temple of God and to build it in three days.'"

Matthew 26:61

"We heard Him say, 'I will destroy this temple made with hands, and within three days I will build another made without hands.'"

Mark 14:58

Jesus answered and said to them, "Destroy this temple, and in three days I will raise it up."

John 2:19

---

[5] *Adler, M, "The Emperor Julin and the Jews," JQR, O. S., V (1893), pages 591-651 JE, "Julian the Apostate*

This should speak volumes to those who believe God supports the temple model that He used in the past. Each of us is designed to be "the temple" of God. We must devote our life in preparing our body, soul and mind for God through His Spirit to control us. We must trust God to demonstrate His resting place inside us and not a "church" building.

The Body of Christ is His Church and we should meet to celebrate the risen Christ on the streets, in buildings, restaurants and any place the Holy Spirit leads.

In the pages to come we will explore together the subtle ways the spirit of deception has captured those who love Jesus but have been taught wrongly.

This is not a book to condemn but to enlighten. I started in the same system and only by the mercy and grace of God have I begun to understand the depths of liberty Christ Jesus has obtained for all creation.

Unfortunately, the Jewish Jesus of Nazareth is the only one portrayed to believers in most churches. Therefore, because of this, He is depicted as only partially finishing His work on earth because those who crucified Him are still waiting on their Messiah. But as we explore the scriptures, The Spirit of Truth will rip away the veils and reveal The Resurrected Christ who has finished the work.

I have shown your glory on earth; I have finished the work you gave me to do

John 17:4 TEV

Chapter 3

THE MODERN DAY GALATIA CHURCH

"Foolish Galatians, who has bewitched you not to obey the truth, before whose eyes Jesus Christ was openly set forth among you as crucified?

I only want to learn this from you: Did you receive the Spirit by the works of the law or by hearing with faith?

Are you so foolish? After beginning with the Spirit, are you now going to be made complete by the flesh?"

Galatians 3:1-3 WEB

The spirit that bewitched them is the same spirit that crucified Christ and it is the same anti-Christ spirit today that has blinded the hearts and minds of the leaders in most churches.

The Greek word for *witchcraft* is baskaino, which means slander or cast a spell upon; to bewitch by words, to enchant. (mala lingua nocere, Virg. Ecl. vii. 28), (Bos, Exercitatt. page 173 f. and Wetstein)[6]

During the time of Paul, there was a group of people known as Judaizers whose life was dedicated to harass the Disciples of Christ. This was accomplished by teaching that for God to accept the Gentiles they must conform to the Mosaic Law, including circumcision. In other words, Non-Jews must become Jewish proselytes first before they could follow Christ. That mentality still exists today in many places.

The supernatural display of God delivering Israel from Egypt was the most persuasive argument used to convince people. This made the new converts doubt the message of grace and follow the Law. This was the seduction of the anti-Christ spirit or witchcraft.

Paul was very familiar with witchcraft having had to cast out these spirits in nearly every town he traveled. Moreover, during his time, there were stories that describe sorcerers who possessed the power to hypnotize people to believe their suggestions through their magical gaze. These people were said to have an "evil eye", whose enchanting gaze could control ones mind. So, Paul asked, who are these evil sorcerers who are hypnotizing you Galatians, to believe the Law over Christ?

Paul was warning the "believers" in Galatia not to follow

---

[6] *Heinrich August Wilhelm Meyer's NT Commentary,*
http://biblehub.com/commentaries/galatians/3-1.htm

the Old Testament Laws and feasts that were only a shadow of Christ but rather to trust The Holy Spirit through faith. Paul reminds them in his letter that Abraham was counted righteous before The Law because of his faith.

The power of witchcraft is the ability to convince one to believe a lie, and its purpose is to control that person with fear.

The Law was given to reintroduce the world to the Heavenly Father and prepare the way for all creation to meet Him through Christ.

> *"All things are delivered to me by my Father; and no one knows who the Son is but the Father, nor who the Father is but the Son, and he to whom the Son may choose to reveal Him."*
>
> *Luke 10:22 WEY*

The power of faith is the knowledge of Christ. That understanding is both the blueprint and purpose of God's Kingdom. The authority of knowing who you are and why you are here is the freedom that removes fear and transforms the future generations.

The Bible says men love darkness more than light because their deeds are evil. The birth, death and resurrection of Jesus as The Christ removed the authority of the devil as the ruler of this world. satan's hypnotic, bewitching rulership was ended but not the lies he had woven through religious doctrines and traditions.

Most churches today would rather follow traditions and doctrines than to pursue the uncharted courses of the prophetic and spiritual dimensions. This practice has produced the sad spiritual condition of most believers today, which is to depend on another person's interpretation of the Bible rather than to pursue The Spirit.

Most leaders of the mainstream denominations are taught to believe, without question, the historical doctrinal interpretations of the scriptures. These erroneous teachings are responsible for the sin consciousness in the world because they deny the authority and power of Christ, beginning with the lie of Good Friday and Easter Sunday.

> *For as Jonah was three days and three nights in the belly of the great fish, so will the Son of Man be three days and three nights in the heart of the earth.*
> *Matthew 12:40*

The practice of celebrating a Friday crucifixion and Sunday resurrection has single handedly destroyed the authority of Christ. They don't deny He was resurrected but they do in essence call Him a liar, because He told them He would be in the heart of the earth three days and three nights, not two days and nights.

My definition of witchcraft is to mix the truth with a lie. Compromising the truth of Christ to believe a pagan tradition is witchcraft.

Thus the churches that do this, even if it is by ignorance, are practicing witchcraft every spring by following this tradition. The controlling power behind witchcraft is fear. That is why those who practice this tradition have no faith to combat the circumstances of this world, which are rooted in fear. This deception must be recognized for what it is and then renounced. The power over fear is faith, which is the result of knowing God.

If the church will not believe Christ, then the earth will cry out, in the forms of wars, droughts, famines, diseases and other catastrophic events. The verses in Luke describe the earth's recognition of its creator.

> *They shouted joyfully, "Blessed is the king who comes in the name of the Lord! Peace in heaven, and glory in the highest heaven."*
>
> *Some of the Pharisees in the crowd said to Jesus, "Teacher, tell your disciples to be quiet."*
> *Jesus replied, "I can guarantee that if they are quiet, the stones will cry out."*
>
> *Luke 19:38-40 GW*

For example, the storm that was sinking the ship carrying Jonah was not because of the idolaters on board the ship but rather because Jonah was refusing to obey God. The condition of the world today is because of the consciousness of the church, which has been corrupted by the spirit of witchcraft.

> *"If anyone listens to my sayings, and doesn't believe, I don't judge him. For I came not to judge the world, but to save the world."*
> *John 12:47 WEB*

> *"He who rejects me, and doesn't receive my sayings, has one who judges him. **The word that I spoke, the same will judge him in the last day.**"*
>
> *John 12:48 WEB*

Jesus was not sent to judge the world, but to save it because the words He spoke would do that by removing unrighteousness. As you will learn later in this book, Jesus is both the seventh day and The Lord of the Sabbath.

God set aside the seventh day for Himself and all those who would enter His rest. The "last day" spoken about in verse 48 refers to our recognizing that God made six days for man to discover Christ.

The "last day" defines our transition from the law to the Spirit. In other words, our rejection of the witchcraft that has stripped our faith is the last day we remain bound to, the law of sin and death.

The resurrection of Christ on the Sabbath Day is the reality of God returning man back to the Garden.

A thorough re-study of the scriptures through the eyes of God's Spirit will enlighten us to the massive seduction and bewitching that has taken place in most Christian churches. The errors begin with elementary truths that have been twisted, such as His crucifixion and the experience we call "born again".

> *"It is **in Him**, and through the shedding of His blood, that we have our deliverance — the*

forgiveness of our offences — so abundant was God's grace,

*... For I always beseech the God of our Lord Jesus Christ — the Father most glorious — to give you **a spirit of wisdom and revelation through an intimate knowledge of Him**, the eyes of your understanding being enlightened so that you may know **what is the hope which His call to you inspires**, what the wealth of the glory of His inheritance in God's people, and what the transcendent greatness of His power in us believers as seen in the working of His infinite might when He displayed it in Christ by raising Him from the dead and **seating Him at His own right hand** in the heavenly realms, high above all other government and authority and power and dominion, and every title of sovereignty used either in **this Age or in the Age to come**.*

*   **God has put all things under His feet**, *and has appointed Him universal and supreme* **Head of the Church, which is His Body**, *the completeness of Him who everywhere **fills the universe with Himself**."*

Ephesians 1:7 & 17-23 WEY

The Spirit of God is speaking volumes through these few verses. If we only understood one tenth of what is being said, everything we read in the scriptures would change dramatically.

Paul uses the prepositional phrase *"IN HIM"* over 25 times; depending on what translation you use, to describe the position of those who are the Body of Christ.

This position can only be achieved through a "new birth" as Jesus described to Nicodemus. This is not a salvation experience that has been so widely believed and preached. (For a greater understanding of this experience consult the First Volume of this series entitled the *"The Last Adam"*.)

Notice the verse that says, *"God has put all things under His feet."* That fulfills what David spoke about in Psalms.

> *THE LORD (God) says to my Lord (the Messiah), Sit at My right hand, until I make Your adversaries Your footstool.*
> *Psalms 110:1 AMP*

King Jesus put all things under His feet and He is waiting on each of us to enter Him, as His Body, in order to enjoy the dominion that He has achieved.

> *"The scepter or leadership shall not depart from Judah, nor the ruler's staff from between his feet, until Shiloh [the Messiah, the Peaceful One] comes to Whom it belongs, and to Him shall be the obedience of the people".*
> *Genesis 49:10 AMP*

The verse in Genesis should enlighten those who believe Jesus must return to establish rulership and acceptance from those who crucified Him. This deception began in Galatia and has been perpetuated throughout time. Jesus received the scepter as Christ and is the King of Kings now and forevermore. He is waiting on us to understand the fullness of what He achieved.

Jesus will not live your life for you. That is why He gave us free will. However, if we listen and follow His Spirit we can live free from fear, which is uncommon among most of those who profess Christ today.

The Spirit of Wisdom has an assignment. That assignment is to reveal the resurrected Christ and His Kingdom. Anyone who follows traditions or has a preconceived image, idea and doctrine of Christ will have a difficult time hearing the truth.

Those who mentally and spiritually pursue the living Christ will experience a dimensional shift from a position of *"waiting"* to *"knowing."* The power of that transition destroys the past and reveals both the knowledge and purpose of your life.

God created us to know Him personally while still alive physically. These encounters awaken our spirits, which remind us of our origins from inside The Father of all spirits.

> *Let the LORD, the God of the spirits of all flesh, set a man over the congregation,*
>
> *Numbers 27:16*

All parents, with more than one child, must constantly guard against appearing to favor one over the other. Nevertheless, some children find a way into the hearts of their parents much faster than does their siblings. I believe our Heavenly Father reacts in a similar fashion. For example, why did God allow Enoch to return to Him without experiencing death?

In my opinion, the intensity of his pursuit of God pleased the Father so much that He decided that Enoch had met his requirements on earth. Maybe the Father is still looking for those who will touch Him the way Enoch did. Does that mean I believe we do not have to die physically? I'm not saying that, but there is nothing impossible for those who believe.

I do believe that after the flood physical death was much different than after Christ's resurrection. Those who have intimate knowledge of Christ today do not have to fear death. Jesus rarely spoke about physically dying.
In fact, He said, let the dead bury the dead implying those who "know" Christ are resurrected now even though they are walking around in a physical body.

> *"I assure you, most solemnly I tell you, if anyone observes My teaching [lives in accordance with My message, keeps My word], he will by no means ever see and experience death."*
>
> *John 8:51 AMP*

The more acquainted we become with Him the less likely we are to believe interpretations from the scriptures that are contrary to our personal experiences and knowledge of Him.

It doesn't matter where you are or where you have been in your search to know Him. His plan for you is perfect. My goal is to both encourage and provoke you in that process.

Each of us must have the courage to challenge both our beliefs and their foundations. If you are willing to change after discovering the truth, your future will be extraordinary.

> *No one can please God without faith, for whoever comes to God must have faith that God exists and rewards those who seek him.*
>
> *Hebrews 11:6 TEV*

There can be no true encounter without first recognizing that He is God. Our belief that He IS ALL IN ALL creates a conduit of communication.

Then, because He is our Heavenly Father, His interaction with us can resemble the way we interact with our children. Each one is special but different. God chooses the way He relates with His creation, and words rarely describe the full impact of such visitations.

Jesus always challenged the beliefs of His disciples. In fact at one point He told them, *"If this is too hard for you then you can leave me as well."* (paraphrasing *John 6:67*)

Most all of us have accepted the picture of a historical Jesus that occurred in a specific time in history. However, time and history cannot capture or describe what happened after His resurrection. This is where eternity begins and history ends.

Jesus is ever ascending to His Father who is above all things. That makes everything that pertains to Christ spiritual not historical.

"And I, if I am lifted up from the earth, will draw all people to myself."

John 12:32 WEB

Those who want to belong to Him must meet Him above the earth not on it.

Chapter 4

Foundations

My journey to find the truth has taken me through many dark, lonely and frightening months that challenged my core beliefs. I never doubted that Jesus was the Son of God and had sacrificed His sinless life for me. Those truths were irrevocable to me but the details concerning His death, resurrection and future reign, I wanted to know directly from The Spirit of God.

One day the Holy Spirit asked me the following questions that could be helpful for you to answer as well. Are you courageous enough to discover Christ for yourself, even if it requires renouncing what you have been taught?

My answer was and still remains to be yes, because the revelation of Christ is ever ascending and His achievements will require eternity to understand. Anyone who tells you differently has stopped pursuing Him.

Before you answer that question consider this, do you think your eternal home should be decided from the interpretations and revelations of others?

Of course the answer to that question is no. Nevertheless, all of us have relied on others for their opinions and advice as it pertains to Biblical interpretations. There is nothing wrong with that except when it pertains to one's personal relationship with Christ.

Each of us must have a personal encounter with the resurrected Christ and His definitive victory over death and satan. That means we should know His role in fulfilling the Law as our Passover Lamb intimately. Otherwise, we will submit to traditions and theologies that will control us with the spirit of fear, which is the power of religion.

In other words, each person is responsible for understanding the precise way He conquered death and completed His assignment that destroyed the kingdom of fear, death and hell. That knowledge is the key to your victory in the flesh and promotion in God's Kingdom.

It will take courage to trust the Holy Spirit for that knowledge. The truth will not be found in most mainstream evangelical thinking. Nevertheless, faith will be the result of your discovering the truth and it will open greater revelation to those with the fortitude to trust the Holy Spirit.

My decision to find the truth has cost me but the price is nothing compared to the joy of knowing Him. My relationship with the Holy Spirit is unimaginable and I have learned that there is no fear for those who remain in His presence. He trusts me with the Mysteries of the Kingdom and He continues to take me into places and subjects that have been the most difficult to understand.

The only thing He requires from me is to trust Him enough to remove my preconceived ideas and doctrines.

Your willingness to forsake your religious clichés and challenge your core beliefs will open heaven over your life. The more innocently you approach Him the more truth you will receive.

I'm not suggesting you exchange one doctrine for another or follow another "man's interpretation". I am asking you to divorce yourself from preconceived ideas and interpretations and allow the Spirit of God to teach you "The Truth."

> *But when He, the Spirit of Truth (the Truth-giving Spirit) comes, He will guide you into all the Truth (the whole, full Truth). For He will not speak His own message [on His own authority]; but He will tell whatever He hears [from the Father; He will give the message that has been given to Him], and He will announce and declare to you the things that are to come [that will happen in the future].*
>
> *John 16:13 AMP*

Each of us are responsible for our own revelation not just the pastors and leaders we have trusted for our spiritual life. The power of Christ is formed from the knowledge of knowing Him and what He finished.

There is no power in trusting people's interpretations of what they believe will happen in the future. Knowing the resurrected Christ is the spiritual truth that transcends time **because everything He did was completed before the foundation of the world.**

If a person's foundation as a Christian is built on a theology or another person's interpretation it will not support the manifold wisdom of God. That understanding is spiritual and cannot be learned from man's reasoning, which is constructed from fear and misconception.

> *... that there might be made known now to the principalities and the authorities in the heavenly [places], through the assembly,* ***the manifold wisdom of God,***
> *Ephesians 3:10 YNG*

> ***The purpose is that through the church the complicated, many-sided wisdom of God in all its infinite variety and innumerable aspects might now be made known to the angelic rulers and authorities (principalities and powers) in the heavenly sphere.***
> *Ephesians 3:10 AMP*

The wisdom Paul is speaking about is the spiritual power released by the reality of what Christ finished before the foundation of the world.

Each generation is responsible to discover for themselves the finished work of Christ. That spiritual knowledge is the power that removes the powers and principalities that are ruling during their time span on earth.

In other words, every person born on the planet encounters the powers and principalities ruling their region because the previous inhabitants were blinded to the completed work of Christ. The wisdom of God, in Christ, destroyed the authority of that demonic kingdom and replaced it with His Kingdom. But that spiritual Kingdom must be made visible through our reality of Christ. This is achieved by establishing on earth what is in heaven.

The reality of what Christ did was made manifest in both the visible and invisible realms. That reality requires the revelation of Christ that can only be achieved through a personal encounter. Spiritual truth is not found in doctrines, religious formulas or rituals. The reality of Christ is only encountered spiritually and then worked out through the mind of Christ.

Jesus expresses this in the following verse:

> *"Don't you believe that **I am in the Father and the Father is in me**? What I'm telling you doesn't come from me. **The Father, who lives in me, does what he wants.**"*
> *John 14:10 GWord*

In the beginning, God created Adam as a spiritual being with the mind of God and a physical body. Today, because of Adam's sin, man is born as a physical being with a mind totally void and disconnected from The Spirit of God.

This is one reason it is so difficult for man to understand the spiritual language used by Christ. More importantly, this is precisely why people rely on others to interpret the Bible for them.

The last Adam, as Paul calls him, is a life giving spirit, which means Jesus of Nazareth had completed His assignment in the physical world by giving mankind access to The Spirit of God once again.

And so it is said, The first man Adam was a living soul. The last Adam is a life-giving spirit.

1 Corinthians 15:45 BBE

Simply put, Christ returned the Kingdom of God to earth and enabled man to reconnect with The Father by The Spirit. The resurrected man, Jesus The Christ, had replaced the Law of Moses with the spiritual Kingdom of God, or The New Covenant.

God's grace, in the person of Christ opened heaven and condemned satan for eternity. Paul, the most prolific writer concerning faith, says something extremely important in Ephesians 2:

Because by grace you have salvation through faith; *and that not of yourselves: God gives it:*

Ephesians 2:8 BBE

Jesus, "The Grace" had pardoned all of mankind so He could now unveil The Truth of both His spiritual nature and authority over evil.

For the Law was given through Moses; **grace and truth came through Jesus Christ.**

John 1:17 WEY

Chapter 5

Word Of Faith

My introduction and education on faith came from either reading or hearing sermons of renowned men of God such as, *Smith Wigglesworth, Kenneth Hagin, Kenneth Copeland* and *Charles Capps*.

I was fascinated by these messages because for the first time I felt as if the Bible was relevant and could solve my day-to-day problems. In fact, one of the faith magazines was called the *"Voice of Victory Magazine."*

Each of these ministries taught what came to be known as *"the word of faith message."* These sermons introduced the *"sowing and reaping principles"* as one of the necessary actions to activate ones faith. We were all instructed that *"sowing a seed"* in the form of finances would facilitate faith.

These messages subtly taught that giving money would empower God to answer the faith of the person giving.

The teaching made sense to me because I was not a giver and although tithing was taught in my church, giving money was not an easy thing for me to do. Therefore, if it was the secret to moving God on my behalf, I wanted to try it.

I started out by giving or "sowing" $100 to one of the ministries teaching me their interpretation of faith and within weeks of my sowing money, a blessing of some sort would take place. The blessing came in the form of financial increase or an opportunity to enhance my quality of life.

The more I followed the prosperity teachers, as they became known, the more aggressive I was with my giving. On a number of occasions I gave thousands of dollars and within several weeks what I gave was multiplied many times over. This convinced me to believe that the message was both approved by God and the solution for my financial lack. But later I started to question if it was really faith that was producing the increase?

I understood from the scriptures that faith both pleased God and is the invisible power that created the physical dimension. In fact, the faith teachers quoted Hebrews and Romans extensively. They cited Romans 10:17 as one of the key's for increasing ones faith.

> *So faith comes from hearing, and hearing by the word of God.*
>
> *Romans 10:17*

My interpretation of what they taught was, that if you read the scriptures out loud your faith would increase. This was a method for memorizing the "word" so it could be spoken or confessed over the circumstances that he or she wanted to change. For example, those who were frightened or fearful would quote the following verses:

> *There is no fear in love, but perfect love casts out fear; for fear has to do with punishment, and whoever fears has not reached perfection in love.*
>
> *1 John 4:18 NRSVS*

> *Little children, you are from God, and have conquered them; for the one who is in you is greater than the one who is in the world.*
>
> *1 John 4:4 NRSVS*

> *But no weapon will be able to hurt you; you will have an answer for all who accuse you. I will defend my servants and give them victory." The LORD has spoken.*
>
> *Isaiah 54:17*

Moreover, those wanting to prosper financially, which were the largest part of those who followed the teachings, would quote these scriptures:

> *Pray for the peace of Jerusalem: May those who love you prosper.*
>
> *Psalm 122:6 TEV*

> *But my God shall supply all your need according to his riches in glory by Christ Jesus.*
>
> *Philippians 4:19*
>
> *Beloved, I wish above all things that thou may prosper and be in health, even as your soul prospers.*
>
> *3 John 2 WEY*

The following scripture was at the heart of the "faith" message and was said to be the key to changing ones circumstances:

> *...in the presence of Him whom he believed — God, who gives life to the dead and calls those things which do not exist as though they did;*
>
> *Romans 4:17*

> *...as the scripture says, "I have made you father of many nations." So the promise is good in the sight of God, in whom Abraham believed — the God who brings the dead to life and whose command brings into being what did not exist.*
>
> *Romans 4:17 TEV*

Confessing or calling things that were not visible, such as finances, while sowing money was the method most often illustrated to produce a harvest of money.

In other words, the students of the faith message were taught to confess prosperity and plant or sow a financial seed in faith, in order to reap a monetary harvest.

The illustration of planting wheat seed to produce a harvest of wheat was used as the model to describe sowing money to reap money. Furthermore, if one planted a seed, in the form of money into good ground, which was represented by that particular minister, that seed would produce more money.

Perhaps, one of the most famous word of faith teachers was *Kenneth Hagin*, whose miraculous healing was attributed to his confessing *Mark 11:23-24*:

> *In solemn truth I tell you that if any one shall say to this mountain, 'Remove, and hurl thyself into the sea,' and has no doubt about it in his heart, but steadfastly believes that what he says will happen, it shall be granted him.*
>
> *That is why I tell you, as to whatever you pray and make request for,* ***if you believe that you have received it, it shall be yours.***
>
> *Mark 11:23-24 WEY*

There is no doubt Jesus understood how to change the physical world with His faith. Nevertheless, Jesus explains the source of His faith and the substance behind His Words. He says, **have faith in God** (*Mark 11:22*).

Sadly, more often than not, my faith was in those teaching me faith, not in God. **My trust was in their success not in my relationship with God.** In short, I had faith in *"their faith."* I did not have an intimate knowledge of God, who is the origin of all things.

Chapter 6

Have Faith In God

" Jesus said to them, have faith in God."

Mark 11:22

During one of my encounters with the Lord He asked me why I thought most of my prayers weren't answered, even when I concluded by saying, in Jesus name?" Before I could answer I heard Him say clearly,

"The Father answers prayers of faith and those who use the name of Jesus must believe that He completed the work of the Father."

That response shook my foundational understanding of faith and challenged my interpretations of the scriptures.

The bottom line was this: **Most of my personal beliefs concerning the Bible were from those who had themselves been taught by others.** This was especially true as it pertained to faith.

My faith or belief was literally formed from the teachings and the thinking of others. The truth was, my trust was in the men and women who taught the message of faith.

Unfortunately, that same principle was true for most of my beliefs about the Bible, especially concerning the prophetic interpretation of the scriptures.

God is faith and those who have a desire to search the deeper things of life will encounter the invisible realm that will both challenge their trust and security in the visible world. This is where the real journey begins for people. The choice will eventually be on whether to follow man and religion or discover God through the power of faith.

My encounter with the spiritual dimensions of God was after being exposed to religious teachings and doctrines. I encountered the resurrected Christ, as "The Living Word" after becoming determined to discover Him for myself. The scriptures were no longer two-dimensional words but they literally became alive.

The Bible was God's DNA and no longer a mysterious book that was too difficult to understand. It was alive and began to resonate or speak to my spirit. The Faith of God activated my spirit and opened dimensions of heaven like never before.

> *We belong to God. The person who knows God listens to us. Whoever doesn't belong to God doesn't listen to us.* ***That's how we can tell the Spirit of truth from the spirit of lies.***
> *1 John 4:6 GWord*

The scriptures in John made it clear to me that God made each person responsible for His or Her relationship with Christ. I was responsible for my relationship with the living Christ, not the pastor, prophet, teacher, apostle, or whatever title of the person who had taught me the Bible.

Therefore, it was first and foremost my assignment to find the Kingdom of God according to the words of Jesus. *"Seek first the kingdom of God and His righteousness… …"* (*Matthew 6:33*). I knew that anything that pertained to understanding the scriptures required both faith and The Spirit of Truth.

> *But without faith it is impossible to please Him, for he who comes to God must believe that He is, and that He is a rewarder of those who diligently seek Him.*
>
> *Hebrews 11:6 NKJ*

Faith is the foundation for revelation and without it we cannot please God.

CHRIST PRODUCES FAITH

> *IN THE beginning [before all time] was the Word (Christ), and the Word was with God, and the Word was God Himself*
>
> *John 1:1 AMP*

Faith is the invisible power that produces a shift in what we trust in the natural world. That experience dramatically alters our perception of reality by eliminating our five senses as the litmus test for what we believe.

Jesus was the Word, before time, which means His truth operates independently of physical laws. That eliminates the visible world as THE factor for discerning the truth.

Please reread this last paragraph until your spirit connects with The Word.

Paul wrote that faith came by hearing the word. I was taught that meant to audibly recite Bible scriptures. But if Jesus is the Word, faith must depend on hearing Jesus. In fact, salvation itself depends on hearing The Spirit of God.

The method taught by the word of faith teachers subtly removed the spiritual dimension and emphasized the physical realm by repeating words from a book.

> *... according as He did choose us in him before the foundation of the world, for our being holy and unblemished before Him, in love,*
>
> *Ephesians 1:4 YNG*

Anyone can interpret the scriptures to mean whatever will justify their beliefs. However, if you hear the Spirit of Truth you will awaken to what you knew before the foundation of the world.

The Bible is a spiritual bridge that connects the unseen to the physical world by the Word of Christ. It requires FAITH to both begin and access that spiritual dimension.

But without an encounter with the Word, as Christ, it is impossible to have faith. One may have hope or trust in others, as I did, but until I determined to find the truth for myself, my life as a Christian was empty of substance. Until I had a spiritual awakening with the resurrected Christ, the Bible did not make sense.

> *It is the spirit that gives life; the flesh is useless. The words that I have spoken to you are spirit and life.*
> *John 6:63*

The Word or Christ is the origin from whence all physical laws and life began. It was necessary for Jesus to become the Christ to send the Holy Spirit or Spirit of Truth. The challenge for many is to understand the Word as spiritual and not physical.

The physical reality of Jesus is one thing but the substance of faith is The Christ, and what He finished before time as God's Word.

The physical world operates with laws such as those identified by *Sir Isaac Newton* centuries ago, one being *cause and effect*. That simply means every action produces a reaction, such as sowing and reaping.

Cause and effect does not produce faith but rather it makes one more dependent on the physical world of sowing and reaping. The Law of Moses was designed to teach Israel faith but it made them dependent upon cause and effect, and not the Kingdom of God.

> *The law indeed was given through Moses; grace and truth came through Jesus Christ.*
>
> *John 1:17 NRSV*

Jesus, The Word is both the faith and grace of God. Jesus as The Risen Christ is the source and substance of grace. Otherwise, faith is merely hope in something that may happen in the future.

KNOWING THE RESURRECTED GRACE OF GOD ACTIVATES FAITH

The grace of God is freely given to those who call on the name of the only begotten Son of God. Salvation is the result of that action. **But the mysteries of God are reserved for those who know the truth as Christ.**

Jesus is the door to The Father and grace is the key that activates our faith to pursue the truth. The truth is the knowledge of Christ and can only be taught by The Spirit of Truth.

Faith is required to know Jesus as the truth. Faith in God is the by-product of those who are immersed into Christ. Perhaps, no other verses illustrate the faith in God as much as those in John 14:

> *"Believe me when I say that I am in the Father and the Father is in me. If not, believe because of the things I do.*
> *I am telling you the truth: those who believe in me will do what I do—yes, they will do even*

greater things, because I am going to the Father.
When that day comes, you will know that I am in my Father and that you are in me, just as I am in you."

John 14:11-12; 20 TEV

Jesus performed all of His miracles because He was "IN" The Father. He tells the disciples they will do greater works if they have FAITH in HIM, because He is going back to The Father.

Jesus was in The Father and those who know Him as The Christ have the same faith He had as Jesus on earth. That relationship is only realized through a spiritual birth.

Jesus of Nazareth was both God's Son and the Son of Man. Recognizing the difference between the Son of Man and The Christ is paramount for anyone who wants to experience the reality of Gods Kingdom now.

Jesus of Nazareth finished His assignment in the flesh, in order that the Spirit of Truth could establish the Kingdom of God on earth as it is in heaven.

"And He, when He comes, will make the world conscious of sin, and of righteousness, and of being judged:
*About sin, because they do not **believe in Me**;*

John 16:8-9 BE

Sin is not what you do, it is what you BELIEVE !!! If your faith is in a lie about the work of Christ on the cross, then you can´t have Bible faith.

Knowing the resurrected Christ activates your faith and provokes you to live IN HIM the way He lived in the Father when He was Jesus of Nazareth.

The invisible realm is governed by the sovereignty of God and is referred to as His mysteries. Those mysteries are revealed and shared with those who enter the Kingdom of God through the Spirit of Truth. **That transition requires the faith "in God" that can only be given by Christ.**

> *"He answered, Knowledge of the Mysteries of the Kingdom of God has been granted to you; but to the rest, they are made known through parables so that 'they may look but not see, and hear but not understand."*
>
> *Luke 8:10 NAB*

> *"Thus should one regard us: as servants of Christ and stewards of the Mysteries of God."*
>
> *1 Corinthians 4:1 NAB*

Those who are spiritually born from Jesus into Christ have God's faith and therefore are IN HIM.

That is my definition of "Born Again" spoken about in *John 3*.

There are many people who believe Jesus was God's Son and was crucified for our sins, but have never been born into The Christ. You should ask yourself why?

- If your faith is in someone other than the resurrected Christ then you may have a belief, but as we have said, that is not faith. This is crucial for you to understand. Faith is only released to those who believe what Jesus finished.

- If what you believe is not born from a personal encounter with the Spirit of the Living Christ, then most likely, you are believing a doctrine which has been constructed by the same spirit Paul writes about in Galatians.

I am re-emphasizing that mixing both the spiritual and physical dimensions together creates doctrines and religions, which removes faith and controls people through fear.

The spirit of witchcraft, as Paul named it, seduces people to believe that following the Law or the Old Covenant is holy to God. Consequently, people are controlled by fear and live their lives in bondage.

Church doctrines are constructed to perpetuate dogmas and superstition, which is witchcraft. Christ and His work are the substance of faith that is used to build His Church. God is the author and source of faith, whereas doctrines and denominations are formed with fear.

Most prophetic teachings today are steeped in fear and superstition peddling the lies of a vengeful Jesus, returning to destroy the nations to rescue a "church" that does not demonstrate faith but rather fear.

I for one have had enough of the lies and fearmongering, and choose to believe Peter.

> *Seeing that* **His divine power has granted to us everything pertaining to life and godliness, through the true knowledge of Him** *who called us by His own glory and excellence.*
>
> *2 Peter 1:3 NASB*

Faith is not what we have been taught, but what we experience daily through our encounters with His Spirit.

That is the faith in God that Jesus spoke about in Mark 11. That is the only faith that gives one the authority to know that what we ask for has already been given.

> *Jesus said to them, Have faith in God.*
>
> *Mark 11:22 NET*

Begin now by repenting for trusting in other people's interpretation of YOUR Bible and ask the Holy Spirit to reveal the truth to you. Do not let fear or doubt hinder your pursuit of Christ.

Chapter 7

Faith Is in the Truth of What Christ Did

Corruption of The Truth Originates at the Cross

He said to them in reply, "An evil and unfaithful generation seeks a sign, but no sign will be given it except the sign of Jonah the prophet.
Just as Jonah was in the belly of the whale three days and three nights, so will the Son of Man be in the heart of the earth three days and three nights."
Matthew 12:39-40 NAB

There are specific scriptures that have been used to confound and confuse Christians for hundreds of years. The reason that was so easily accomplished was because Christians followed the pagan ritual of the Good Friday crucifixion and the Sunday resurrection taught by the Roman Catholic Church. It is obvious from the above scripture that following that tradition does not add up to three days and nights.

That is THE fundamental lie that makes all of the false prophetic interpretations so easy to believe. Moreover, it absolutely nullifies Christ as the Messiah, which was why He was crucified.

The strategy behind witchcraft is to seduce one to believe a lie, which allows for the building of false structures in one's life. The greatest weapon is to convince one to use reason rather than faith.

Initially, there is nothing more terrifying than to discover that what you had believed was the truth, is in reality a lie. Notice I said, initially, because after The Holy Spirit reveals the truth those fears and doubts, which supported the lies, will disappear. Consequently, in its place, The Christ emerges in His Glory, and Grace changes the unbelief and fear into faith.

Faith is the substance of the invisible, but the power to believe is formed from individually witnessing the miraculous. Perhaps, you recognize this as the reality of where you find yourself today. You are a living, breathing miracle and the recognition of that will empower your faith to new levels.

The Bible is written to reveal Christ from Genesis to Revelation. The precise timing of our Lord's birth, death and resurrection is confirmation to God's perfection and undeniable proof of His sovereignty.

The truth has no enemies because it is from God. The truth reveals the miraculous and creates the hunger to discover Christ.

The anti-Christ spirit, which John said was already among them, promotes doubt, unbelief and false interpretations. Although subtle, that spirit is active inside those who appear holy but promote fear through the false interpretation of scriptures.

There are many steps involved on the road to discover the truth about Christ. But none so important than to realize the Bible is written as a testimony to the miraculous life of Christ Jesus. **It is NOT written about Israel.**

The whole Bible is prophetically written about Jesus as The Messiah, who is the heart and soul of the scriptures. Anyone who misrepresents that truth is perverting the truth and leading countless millions astray.

Recognizing Christ as God's Passover Lamb is the most significant step in the miraculous journey to know Him. His crucifixion and resurrection are both the cornerstone and the fulfillment of all prophecy determined before the foundation of the world.

The substance for our faith is hidden inside the details of God's prophetic words spoken thousands of years before Jesus completed His assignment. (Reread this last sentence, please.)

Faith is the only thing that pleases God and Jesus is the visible substance of God's faith. The progressive

revelation of Christ is the most spectacular journey anyone will ever undertake because it pleases The Father. Why? Because no one can follow Christ without faith.

God used and still uses His servants the prophets, to plant spiritual seeds in the physical world, in order for them to perpetually unfold the truth of what Christ accomplished before the foundation of the world.

The prophetic is not fortune telling or giving someone "a word". **It is a greater and fresher revelation of The Living Christ**, which is designed to provoke the next generation to higher and greater experiences with The Father.

There can be no foundation formed on a lie and anyone who blindly follows religious traditions, such as the crucifixion on Good Friday, will neither have the faith nor the knowledge of Christ. If we all will make a conscious effort to challenge our belief in every area of our life we can be sure that The Holy Spirit will lovingly correct any wrong thinking.

Each of us must have an encounter with the miraculous or invisible realm for our foundation of faith to form. This is achieved through the revealed or prophetic, which is why it is at the heart of most church controversies.

Christ won the war, but that revelation cannot be understood with a mind that has been mesmerized by illusion. The battle that rages in the minds and hearts of believers originates with the misinterpretation of the crucifixion and resurrection of Christ. The spirit of the anti-Christ perpetuates that lie in most churches throughout the world.

The devil is the master of illusion and his trickery convinced Adam to choose the tree of knowledge. It is also the fuel that perpetuates religion and has hidden the truth these countless ages. But NOW is the time for your eyes to be opened and for the next generation to choose The Truth over a lie.

The most spectacular proof that God is God, is the demonstration of what He did before the foundation of the world through Christ. The genius and wisdom of our heavenly Father is on display throughout the scriptures as He prophetically unfolds the drama for all ages.

The prophetic words establishing the manifestation of Christ are depicted through God's servants *Ezra*, *Nehemiah*, *Isaiah*, *Jeremiah*, *Daniel* and *John*. These prophets accurately described events before they happened in time proving that God left nothing undone.

> *God is not a man, that He should lie, nor a human being, that He should change His mind. Has He said, and will He not do it? Or has He spoken, and will He not make it happen?*
>
> *Numbers 23:19 NET*

God had already planned satan's destruction and He knew those He had chosen, Israel, to birth the Messiah, would choose by their own free will to both reject and kill Him.

The prophetic Word and its fulfillment destroyed satan.

But his lies are available to those who live in unbelief. If men choose this world's system over the finished work of Christ, which is The Kingdom of God, their lives will not change. God created the earth but man chooses his worldview according to his belief.

Chapter 8

THE SPIRIT OF PROPHECY REVEALED

*I bowed at his feet to worship him. But he told me, "Don't do that! I am your coworker and a coworker of the Christians who hold on to the testimony of Jesus. Worship God, because **the testimony of Jesus is the spirit of prophecy!**"*

Revelation 19:10 GW

The testimony of Jesus is the Spirit of Prophecy. What was the heart of His testimony? That He would be crucified and resurrected on the third day. That means if you or I follow a tradition instead of His Word we are no different than those who don't believe the Bible.

That may sound like a strong statement unless you stop to consider that the condition of the world we live in today is the result of believing lies instead of The Truth.

For example, Jesus said it is more blessed to give than to receive. We believe that is true because Jesus never told a lie. However, the world's system rewards those who have large sums of monies, not givers. This is a small example that the system we trust and follow does not adhere to the ways and truth of God.

Spiritual truth is harder to understand for people who believe that reality is discovered from the physical world, in which they live. The result of trusting ones senses for the truth negates the invisible realm of the spirit, which is the foundation for understanding the words and ways of Christ.

Religion is constructed by mixing the visible with the spiritual realm. That is also the formula for witchcraft.

In other words, people are more easily seduced by witchcraft when the wisdom of this world is mixed with spiritual passages from the Bible. This is the way theology and doctrines of man are formed.

This bewitching creates a false sense of security, because their foundation is built from someone else's interpretations of scriptures, rather than making the effort to discover the truth from the Holy Spirit.

Perhaps, you have heard people say things like, "If there is a God why would He allow catastrophic tragedies such as the Tsunamis'?" Some church folk justify these events with *"end time scenarios"* that are said to happen before the return of Christ. The truth is, the earth is groaning for the Sons of God and this action produces changes that can be violent on the surface and in the oceans. The real answers are discovered after one becomes a Son.

One of the purposes in writing this book is to awaken you to your spiritual origin. Once this happens your opinions and perceptions will surely change. Furthermore, the Holy Spirit will provoke you to revisit the scriptures from a spiritual perspective.

Be encouraged, the Holy Spirit is the master communicator, which means **everyone is capable of understanding the invisible realm if they will first recognize God as Spirit.**

The Bible is the testimony of Christ Jesus and therefore, by reason of the verse in Revelation 19, it must be a spiritual book written from the wisdom of God.

You will notice that John was bowing to an angel that was revealing Christ to him. The question that immediately comes to my mind was, why did this angel have to reveal Christ to the only disciple that knew Jesus better than anyone?

It is obvious that Jesus of Nazareth was not the person John encountered. He saw the glorious Resurrected Christ that was speaking to Him as the ONE that WAS, IS and WILL BE. John was physically experiencing eternity, which has no beginning or ending. You and I are living in eternity right now the same as John revealed in the book of Revelation. Every experience we have should direct us to the Living Christ. Repeat after me: I am a spirit !!!

Jesus was the visible image of God whose earthly life destroyed satan and reestablished God's Kingdom on earth. The fact that it is invisible does not make it any less real or powerful.

People have the right to choose what they believe and either enjoy or suffer the consequences of those choices. The original Adam chose satan, and the world has been suffering the consequences ever since.

The "last Adam" removed satan from controlling man, but not man from choosing to be controlled by satan.

The power of the invisible Kingdom is the authority of God over the illusions of satan, which is what he uses to control our thoughts and beliefs.

We have all seen magic tricks that appear to be real. These are called illusions and that is what magicians use to trick their audiences. Illusionists create myths and fairy tales by disguising a lie to appear true. If you don't know satan was defeated by Christ you will believe his lies.

His greatest illusion is perpetuating the restoration of the Old Covenant by attempting to destroy the reality that Jesus is the Messiah. This was accomplished through "the church" believing Jesus was crucified on Friday and resurrected on Sunday.

Every time *"the church"* celebrates Good Friday as the day He was murdered and Easter Sunday as the day He arose, it denies Jesus as the Messiah. Why? Because He said the only sign that proved He was The Messiah was that of Jonah.

One may think it doesn't matter as long as we celebrate His resurrection. This type of thinking is why the church has not received its rightful inheritance. God will not bestow Sonship to those who do not understand the ways of The King.

The glorious inheritance is awaiting those in the order of the royal priesthood of Melchizedek. The majestic power of this priesthood has been assigned the highest rank in God's Kingdom and for generations God has been waiting on true "Sons" to understand His ways.

The truth is, Jesus said three days and three nights, and what the church is doing by celebrating Friday to Sunday is rejecting His words.

- **Salvation for the Jews began at Passover in Egypt.**

- **The New Covenant started on Passover in Jerusalem for all mankind.**

The timing was just as important for the New Covenant as it was for Moses and The Law.

On the third day He arose and fulfilled ALL the scriptures establishing His Kingdom and overcoming satan. The complete understanding of the prophetic begins with the death and resurrection of Christ Jesus. The following pages are written for you to discover the truth of the Resurrected Christ.

Chapter 9

RESURRECTION DECEPTION

For, as Jonah was in the belly of the fish three days and three nights, so shall the Son of Man be in the heart of the earth three days and three nights.

Matthew 12:40 YNG

One of the most hideous deceptions ever perpetrated on those who love Jesus is the celebration of Easter. **I am not disputing the reality of the crucifixion and resurrection.**

However, the celebration of "Good Friday and Easter Sunday" by the church is, in my opinion, the single most abominable practices that a person of faith could follow.

Remember, mixing the false with the truth is what forms the power of witchcraft. The resurrection of Christ is the spiritual truth. Nevertheless, willfully disregarding His exact timing is tantamount to mixing the truth with a lie, which nullifies the words of Christ.

The supernatural birth, death and resurrection of Christ Jesus was conceived and implemented before the foundation of the world in order to hide it from the devil and even the angels.

I was taught all my Christian life to celebrate "Good Friday" as the day Jesus was crucified and Sunday as the day He resurrected. Like so many others in church, I followed this belief without ever questioning its authenticity.

One day, while reading the Bible, I discovered Jesus comparing His most important achievement as God's son to the time Jonah spent inside the belly of the fish.

> *But He answered them, "An evil and adulterous generation demands a sign, but no sign will be given to it except the sign of the prophet Jonah."*
>
> Matthew 12:39 YNG

> *"For, as Jonah was in the belly of the fish three days and three nights, so shall the Son of Man be in the heart of the earth three days and three nights."*
>
> Matthew 12:40 YNG

The most profound sign that proved Jesus was the Messiah is that of Jonah. The time Jonah was in the belly of the fish was also the time Jesus spent in the heart of the earth. Therefore, it makes no sense to believe a crucifixion on Friday and resurrection on Sunday could equal 72 hours in the heart of the earth.

Here is another fact to consider that makes following that tradition such an abomination. The Jewish Talmud does not consider a person dead if he or she is revived before three days.[7]

Thus, it was considered possible for a soul to reunite with its body within three days, but no more, for sometime on the third day the soul realized the body was rotting, and then departed. A resurrection before the third day might not be a true resurrection, but a mere revival, or the ghost of a not-yet-departed soul, but a resurrection on the third day is true evidence that death was in either sense defeated.

This "*third day tradition*" in Jewish law may in fact be very ancient, possibly lying behind the prophecy of Hosea, "*He will revive us after two days, He will raise us up on the third day, that we may live before him*" (*Hosea 6:2*), and no doubt had something to do with Paul's conviction that Jesus "*was raised on the third day according to the scriptures*" (*1 Corinthians 15:4*).[8]

There is no greater miracle than the resurrection of Christ. The only event that proves Jesus is the Messiah is His

---

[7] *Mishnah, Yebamot 16:3a-e. For examples of this law being cited, cf. Midrash Rabbah, Genesis [LXV:20(595)], [LXXIII:5(669-670)] and Leviticus [XXXIII:5].*

[8] *Richard Carrier, http://infidels.org/kiosk/article/jewish-law-the-burial-of-jesus-and-the-third-day-125.html#23*

death and resurrection after three days, and three nights. Otherwise, He was to be considered a false prophet, as was the indictment by the Pharisee's and Sadducees.

I must admit I was sick to my stomach after recognizing that my following that tradition made me just as guilty as the Jews and Romans in the crucifixion.

No other person ever changed the history of this planet and the future of mankind more than Jesus. His sinless life, death and resurrection were the sacrifice required of Him to fulfill His assignment and reconcile mankind to our Heavenly Father.

This is the cornerstone of our faith. Most of the world believes in a historical Jesus of Nazareth who was crucified and resurrected. The acceptance of that fact is one thing, but the precise and exact way it was achieved is much more important.

A. THE AUTHORITY OVER THE FEAR OF DEATH

We are people of flesh and blood. That is why Jesus became one of us. He died to destroy the devil, who had power over death.

But he also died to rescue all of us who live each day in fear of dying.

Hebrews 2:14-15 CEV

Since the beginning of time man's choices have made him a slave to fear and doubt. Man's decision to trust his physical senses instead of his spirit has produced the darkness that controls his mind.

Faith is the only power over fear and its source is found in the knowledge of the exact way Jesus conquered death. That means we must understand the precision of His birth, death and resurrection.

The world you trust through your senses will dominate you by fear, doubt and unbelief. The Kingdom, that Christ returned to mankind through His resurrection and faith in God destroyed satan's authority and *"the fear of death."*

Our authority over the fear of death depends on our understanding of the exact process Jesus used to dismantle satan's power over mankind.

If our life is to have any power, our belief must be founded on more than a cliché or religious doctrine.

> *"My people are destroyed for lack of knowledge; because you have rejected knowledge, I will also reject you that you shall be no priest to Me; seeing you have forgotten the law of your God, I will also forget your children."*
> *Hosea 4:6 AMP*

The Bible says God's people perish for lack of knowledge. Nothing less than you having a full and immovable knowledge of Jesus as the spotless Lamb of God fulfilling the law, can prepare you for what you were chosen to complete before the foundation of the world.

But what does that mean, *"fulfilling the law?"*

> *This is why people are condemned: The light came into the world. Yet, people loved the dark rather than the light because their actions were evil.*
>
> *People who do what is wrong hate the light and don't come to the light. They don't want their actions to be exposed.*
>
> John 3:19-20 GWord

If you celebrate His death and resurrection on Friday and Sunday respectively, you are in effect saying, that you don't believe He is the Messiah.

Therefore, according to the words of Jesus, if after we learn the truth of His death, burial and resurrection we continue to follow doctrine and tradition, we will through that act, love darkness more than light.

The Law was a shadow of the true Light and nothing hides that Light more profoundly than the traditions of men that we have all followed. The shadow is the darkness Jesus is speaking about in the above verses. Following any religion is darkness because The True Light has come.

It is really more diabolical than you can imagine. One of the best ways to poison someone, undetected, is to begin with a few drops of poison, such as cyanide. Over time the person will die from the cumulative effect of the poison.

That is the way unbelief is introduced into the church. People begin to blindly follow a tradition or doctrine without ever questioning its authenticity. It is shocking to discover the numbers of doctrines that have arisen from not understanding the scriptures. This is especially true as it pertains to the books of Daniel and Revelation.

There is nothing more sinister than to follow man's interpretation of scripture over the words of Christ. This was the sin that condemned the Pharisee's and it may be the one creating the biggest problems in your life.

Because of your traditions you have destroyed the authority of God's word. And you do many other things like that.
Mark 7:13 GWord

B. DOES IT MATTER?

Maybe you don't think it makes a difference whether or not you celebrate a Friday crucifixion and Sunday resurrection. However, if it didn't make any difference why would the scriptures repeat it in so many different ways?

Oh, and by the way, it is mathematically impossible to arrive at 72 hours if one uses a Friday evening crucifixion and Sunday morning resurrection.

"And shall deliver him to the Gentiles to mock, and to scourge, and to crucify him: and the third day he shall rise again."
Matthew 20:19

Command therefore that the sepulcher be made sure until the third day, lest his disciples come by night, and steal him away, and say unto the people, He is risen from the dead: so the last error shall be worse than the first.

Matthew 27:64

For He taught his disciples, and said unto them, "The Son of man is delivered into the hands of men, and they shall kill Him; and after that He is killed He shall rise the third day."

Mark 9:31

"And they shall mock him, and shall scourge him, and shall spit upon him, and shall kill him: and the third day he shall rise again."

Mark 10:34

Saying, "The Son of man must suffer many things, and be rejected of the elders and chief priests and scribes, and be slain, and be raised the third day."

Luke 9:22

And he said unto them, "Go ye, and tell that fox, Behold, I cast out devils, and I do cures today and tomorrow, and the third day I shall be perfected."

Luke 13:32

> *"And they shall scourge him, and put him to death: and the third day he shall rise again."*
>
> *Luke 18:33*

> *Saying, "The Son of man must be delivered into the hands of sinful men, and be crucified, and the third day rise again."*
>
> *Luke 24:7*

> *And said unto them, "Thus it is written, and thus it behooved Christ to suffer, and to rise from the dead the third day."*
>
> *Luke 24:46*

> *"Him God raised up the third day, and showed him openly;"*
>
> *Acts 10:40*

> *"And that He was buried, and that He rose again the third day according to the scriptures."*
>
> *1 Corinthians 15:4*

God is both precise and exact leaving nothing to chance. The most important event to occur on this earth happened exactly the way it was prophesied before the foundation of the world.

Make no mistake about it, every power and principality knows the importance of what Jesus did and the only thing they can do is destroy your faith with doubt and unbelief.

This is perpetuated through the sin-consciousness of the first Adam. God used the Law to trap satan and to introduce Christ. The Law was the shadow of the true Light, Christ Jesus.

If you discover the truth of what, when and how Jesus fulfilled the Law through His crucifixion and resurrection you will be equipped to unlock every prophetic promise in the scriptures. That is how important this understanding is to your future and that of the generations to come.

Accepting pseudo truths, which are lies, will make you miss out in any other prophetic word spoken in the Bible.

C. ORIGIN OF FRIDAY CRUCIFIXION

"It was the so-called "apostolic fathers," in the second century, steeped in pagan traditions, which first began to teach that the crucifixion occurred on Friday. Among them we can quote as St. Ignatius of Antioch, St. Clement, St. Irenaeus, St. Terullian. Yet they admitted that the ancient custom of fasting on Wednesday originated because it was the actual day of the crucifixion[9].

"These same men attempted to disprove Jesus as the Messiah of Israel, beginning with misinformation about His birth, crucifixion and resurrection, creating a great gap between Jesus and His Hebrew roots. They further created confusion with the year He was anointed by the Spirit of The Lord recorded in Luke 4. This was all done to justify a Sunday resurrection of Nimrod the pagan Babylonian God, worshipped by the Romans as Jupiter.

---

[9] *Schaff-Herzog Encyclopedia of Religious Knowledge, "Fasting"*

This false doctrine had no sound biblical proof or authority to rely on, so they resorted to fraudulent tactics to legitimize their fabrications. One such claim was that Hermes, the brother of Pope Pius (about the year AD 47) had received instruction from an angel, who commanded that all men should keep the Pasch [Passover] on the Lord's Day Sunday."[10]

"*Thus, the letter from Hermes was either a forgery or it was deceptively written by Pius, who died just before Polycarp's visit to Rome.*"[11]

The bishops at Rome had decreed that they possessed the power to supersede and change the times and laws of God. They rewrote history and changed the order of events in order to introduce their false doctrines.

Their effort to change the day of the resurrection to Sunday was simply a continuation of the Babylonian tradition — that *Nimrod* (the father of the Babylonian Mystery Religion) was resurrected on a Sunday.

The Roman Emperor *Constantine* established Sunday as part of the official state religion, thus legitimizing all the various traditions attached to that day.

---

[10] *Antiquities of the Christian Church, Joseph Bingham, page 1149*

[11] *Apostolical Fathers, James Donaldson, page 324*

Chapter 10

THE PROPHETIC IS HISTORICALLY PROVEN

There are countless books that historically document the birth of both John The Baptist and Jesus. The power of the prophetic is the key that unlocks the mysteries of the Kingdom to each person, so they may discover their spiritual origin, through Christ.

The Bible is the prophetic record of Christ from Genesis to Revelation. I cannot emphasize this enough. Each person must have a personal encounter with the Spirit of Truth or prophecy, which is Jesus.

The anti-Christ spirit, in conjunction with witchcraft produces fear to control men through religion. However, rest assured the power of this spirit is no match for The Spirit of Truth.

Ignorance, not the devil, is destroying your life, but rejoice: The Spirit of Truth is giving you the authority to take back what has been stolen.

Once this encounter occurred in my life, most of my theology did not make sense any longer, and I can assure you the same will happen to you. This will happen to all those who pursue the reality of Christ for themselves.

The purpose for understanding the dates and times of the birth, life, death and resurrection of Christ is so that our prophetic life becomes more real than our physical senses.

The prophetic word of God destroyed satan beginning in Genesis, but if you don't understand the precise way Jesus used His life to achieve that you will be deceived and unable to discern the truth.

One of the prophetic keys that unlock the scriptures to prove the birth, death and resurrection of Christ begins with the decree to build the temple 483 years before the Birth of Christ.

The Temple was one of the greatest idols of the Jews. Therefore, when Jesus told them He would destroy it and rebuild it in three days, they not only didn't understand Him but it was one of the reasons they wanted to kill Him.

The following accounts are taken from the Restored Church of God. These are tools for you to use in your search to know Christ in an ever-ascending way.

A. THE DECREE OF ARTAXERXES

In the seventh year of Artaxerxes, king of Persia, a decree was made to rebuild Jerusalem (Ezra 7). It followed the decree of Cyrus, in which he acknowledged that the LORD God of Heaven had charged him to build Him a house at Jerusalem, which is in Judah (Ezra 1:2). Artaxerxes' decree was significant because of a prophecy revealed to Daniel.

Daniel states:

> *Know therefore and understand, that from the going forth of the commandment to restore and to build Jerusalem unto the Messiah the Prince shall be seven weeks, and threescore and two weeks: the street shall be built again, and the wall, even in troublous times.*
>
> *Daniel 9:25*

This shows that there are 62 weeks + 7 weeks = 69 prophetic weeks (or 483 days). Applying the *"a-day-for-a-year-principle"* (*Numbers 14:34; Ezekiel 4:6*), we arrive at 483 years from the decree until the beginning of Christ's ministry.

The decree was made during the seventh year of Artaxerxes' reign (457 B.C.). This date is historically well documented. By subtracting 457 from 483, we come to the year A.D. 26.

When counting from B.C to A.D., astronomers correctly add one year since there is no year "zero", while historians and chronologists generally neglect to do this.

Adding one year brings us to A.D. 27 — the prophesied year of the beginning of the ministry of the Messiah.

Luke 3:23 tells us: *"And Jesus Himself began to be about thirty years of age..."* The context of this verse is after John the Baptist had begun his ministry and just before Jesus began His. Since Jesus was 30 years old in A.D. 27, **He would have been born in 4 B.C.**

Remember, we must add one year to compensate for no "zero-year." Thus, advancing 30 years from 4 B.C. brings us to A.D. 27.

This leads us to the next historical proof that further confirms when Christ was born.

B. THE TIME OF HEROD'S DEATH

Shortly after Christ's birth, an angel warned Joseph in a dream that he and his wife Mary were to take the child and flee into Egypt.
They stayed there until the death of Herod (Matthew 2:15). Christ was an infant less than one year of age when Herod died.

Matthew shows that:

> *"Herod slew all the children that were in Bethlehem and, all the coast thereof, from two years old and under, according to the time which he had diligently inquired of the wise men."*
> *Matthew 2:16*

To better establish the exact time of Herod's death, we find in Josephus' Antiquities of the Jews a reference to a lunar eclipse. A footnote in the *Whiston translation of Josephus* states:

"This eclipse of the moon (which is the only eclipse mentioned by Josephus) is of greatest consequence for the determination of the time for the death of Herod... and for the birth and entire chronology of Jesus Christ.

It happened March 13th, in the year of the Julian period[12] 4710, and the 4th year before the Christian era."
(Bk. XVII, ch. vi, sec. 4). According to Josephus, Herod died the following year, 3 B.C.

Soon after Herod's death, the angel instructed Joseph to return to the land of Israel with Mary and Jesus, who would have been about one year old.

C. TIME OF CONSTRUCTION OF THE TEMPLE

As mentioned, Christ was 30 years old (Luke 3:23) when He began His ministry in A.D. 27. Now, we will see how the chronology of the temple harmonizes with the chronology of Christ:

"Then answered the Jews and said unto Him, What sign show You unto us, seeing that You do

---

[12] Julian period, chronological system now used chiefly by astronomers and based on the consecutive numbering of days from Jan. 1, 4713 BC. Not to be confused with the Julian calendar, the Julian period was proposed by the scholar Joseph Justus Scaliger in 1583 and named by him for his father, Julius Caesar Scaliger.

these things? Jesus answered and said unto them, Destroy this temple, and in three days I will raise it up. Then said the Jews, Forty and six years was this temple in building, and will You rear it up in three days? But He spoke of the temple of His body."

John 2:18-21

This occurred on the first Passover during Christ's ministry, in A.D. 28. The Jews said that the temple had been under construction for 46 years. By adding one year to compensate for no "zero-year" this means that the temple's construction began in 19 B.C., the 18th year of Herod's reign.

In *"**Antiquities**"*, Josephus wrote, *"And now Herod, in the eighteenth year of his reign... undertook a very great work, that is to build of himself the temple of God..."* (Bk. XV, ch. xi, sec. 1). From 19 B.C., we advance 46 years since the beginning of the reconstruction of the temple, arriving at A.D. 28 — the first Passover after the beginning of Christ's ministry.

D. THE REIGN OF EMPEROR TIBERIUS

Other historical evidence involves the time of the beginning of John the Baptist's ministry. Luke 3:1 begins, "Now in the fifteenth year of the reign of Tiberius Caesar, Pontius Pilate being governor of Judea..." It then describes the beginning of John's ministry.

The reign of Roman Emperor Tiberius began about A.D. 11 or 12, since he reigned concurrently with

Augustus Caesar for about 2 years. If we add the 15 years of Tiberius' reign to A.D. 11 or 12, we arrive at A.D. 26 or 27 (Luke 3:1-3).

Here again we see the biblical chronology verified by history. ***The 15th year of Tiberius brings us precisely to the beginning of John the Baptist's ministry, which was just before the time of Christ's ministry*** *(emphasis by L. Emerson Ferrell).*

E. THE GOVERNORSHIP OF PONTIUS PILATE

Historians agree that Pilate ruled for ten years. *Luke 3:1* shows that during the 15th year of Tiberius' reign, Pilate was governor. Some historical accounts, such as the Encyclopedia Britannica, date Pilate's rule from A.D. 26 to 36.

When he was recalled, he immediately sought help from his close political ally, Emperor Tiberius. Yet, while Pilate was en route to confer with him, Tiberius died, in A.D. 37. With Tiberius' death, Pilate's rule ended the same year. Therefore, Pilate's ten-year rule would have had to coincide with the years A.D. 27 to 37[13]

Now let's recap:

Pilate's governorship over Judea began in early A.D. 27, during the 15th year of Tiberius' rule.

---

[13] *http://rcg.org/articles/ccwnof.html#*
© 2015 The Restored Church of God.

Meanwhile, John the Baptist began his ministry in early A.D. 27, which preceded Christ's ministry by several months.

Christ's ministry would not have begun until the autumn of A.D. 27 since:

1. He was 30 years old when His ministry began

2. Jesus was born in the autumn of 4 B.C. His ministry could not have begun later than A.D. 28 because, at that point, the temple's 46-year construction would have been finished.

Thus, the autumn of A.D. 27 corresponds with numerous secular and historical proofs, as well as Scripture.

Let's continue with the sequence we were following.

F. DANIEL PROPHECY REVEALED

Remember the prophecy in *Daniel 9:27*, which established 483 years, from 457 B.C. to A.D. 27. Verse 27 establishes the length of Christ's prophesied ministry:

> *And He shall confirm the covenant with many for one week: and in the midst of the week He shall cause the sacrifice and the oblation to cease, and for the overspreading of abominations He shall make it desolate, even until the consummation, and that determined shall be poured upon the desolate.*
>
> *Daniel 9:27*

Christ was to confirm the covenant for one week. According to the "a-day-for-a-year-principle", the seven days of that week equal seven years. Yet, in the midst of the week, the Messiah was to cause the sacrifice and oblations to cease. This was done by offering His own life to cover the sins of all humanity, as part of God's Plan of salvation. The Messiah was *"cut off"* (Verse 26) in the "midst of the week" — after 3½ "days", or prophetic years. His earthly ministry lasted precisely 3½ years.

Then He was cut off — crucified — in the middle of the week — Wednesday. In this prophecy, the "midst of the week" had a dual meaning, as does most prophecy. Since Christ's ministry began in the autumn of A.D. 27, this means that He was crucified in the spring of A.D. 31, 3½ years later."[14]

Prophecy is fulfilled in time, but your choice to believe it is the only thing that will activate its authority in your life. Jesus is the fulfillment of prophecy both physically and spiritually from Genesis through Revelation. He has left nothing undone. Those who do not believe in His finished work are incapable of understanding His authority over their circumstances. Furthermore, they will disqualify themselves as His disciple.

The timing of His birth, death and resurrection are documented through out the scriptures and verified by a Jerusalem born historian named *Titus Flavius Josephus*. Those who want to study the history of those times Jesus prophesied would come after His departure, should read

---

[14] *http://rcg.org/articles/ccwnof.html#*
© *2015 The Restored Church of God*

Josephus' books *"The war of the Jews"* that describes in detail the destruction of Jerusalem in 70 AD.

The most outstanding proof that God left nothing undone was achieved through the cross. satan destroyed himself by walking into the prophetic trap set for him by God in the Garden of Eden.

God is always looking for those who, like His Son, will believe what they cannot see, to become a sign and wonder to the visible world.

G. THE PASSOVERS DURING THE TIME OF JESUS

In order for Jesus to fulfill The Law, which includes all the Feasts, He would need to die precisely on Nisan 14 in the year 31 AD. This required Jesus to attend three Passover Feasts and be crucified as our Passover Lamb at the fourth and final Passover. I said final because He fulfilled the Law. There is no need to continue to follow what God finished.

Incidentally, here is a fascinating fact that also indicates that the resurrection occurred in 31 AD and was recorded in the writings of Josephus, this first century Jewish historian.

He says, the last Jubilee that was celebrated in the land (before the Roman conquest in 70 AD) began in the fall of 27 AD. That date most likely marks the beginning of Jesus' ministry, for His ministry was a symbolic fulfillment of the Jubilee promises.

The scripture indicates this that Jesus read in the synagogue in Nazareth when He launched His public ministry (*Luke 4 & Isaiah 61*):

> *The Spirit of the Lord is upon Me, Because He anointed Me to preach the Gospel to the poor. He has sent Me to proclaim release to the captives, And recovery of sight to the blind, To set free those who are downtrodden, To proclaim the favorable year of the Lord.*
> *Luke 4:16-24 & Isaiah 61:1-2*

It is commonly agreed that the ministry of Jesus lasted 3½ years. A launching date in the fall of 27 AD, to coincide with the beginning of the Jubilee, would place His death in the spring of 31 AD - the year in which the Passover week had two Sabbaths[15].

There is some discussion as to the Bible scripture that describes the last Passover Jesus attended before His crucifixion. But there is no doubt Jesus lived 3½ years after His baptism in Galilee.

The following accounts in the scriptures describe three Passover Feasts.

John records the first Passover of His ministry in A.D. 28:

> *Now when He was in Jerusalem at the Passover, in the feast day, many believed in His name, when they saw the miracles, which He did.*
> *John 2:23*

---

[15] http://www.raptureready.com/featured/reagan/dr14.html

Afterward, Christ began teaching in the area of Judea near Jerusalem.

Luke records an event during the Passover season in the second year of His ministry, in A.D. 29, which also places Jesus in Galilee during this Passover Feast:

> *And it came to pass on the second Sabbath after the first, that He went through the corn fields; and His disciples plucked the ears of corn, and did eat, rubbing them in their hands.*
>
> *Luke 6:1*

The term, *"the second Sabbath after the first"* means the second high day, which was the Day of Unleavened Bread. Although this event is covered in Matthew 12:1-8 and Mark 2:23-28, only Luke's account, written in Greek, makes clear which Sabbath this was. The Greek term, *"deuteroproton sabbaton"*, literally means *"the second Sabbath of the first rank"* — or **the second high day of that Passover season.**

John records the following, which preceded the third Passover (A.D. 30) of Christ's ministry:

> *And the Passover, a feast of the Jews, was near. When Jesus then lifted up His eyes, and saw a great company come unto Him, He said unto Philip, Where shall we buy bread that these may eat?*
>
> *John 6:4-5*

The fourth and final Passover of Christ's ministry is the most documented Passover of all. All four of the gospels cover it in detail. Notice Luke's Version:

> *Now the feast of unleavened bread drew near, which is called the Passover. And the chief priests and scribes sought how they might kill Him; for they feared the people.*
>
> Luke 22:1-2

John records,

> *And the Jews' Passover was near at hand: and many went out of the country up to Jerusalem before the Passover, to purify themselves.*
>
> John 11:55

Christ's final Passover completed His earthly ministry of 3½ years. Again, it began in the autumn of A.D. 27 and ended in the spring of A.D. 31, on a Wednesday—in the midst of the week. (Quoted from *Daniel 9:27*)

The majority of the Christian world claims that Christ's crucifixion occurred on a Friday, in A.D. 33.

Below is an article by *Herman L. Hoeh* that documents the Jewish calendar during the time of Jesus:

"Here is the chart, which can be verified by any work on the "Jewish Calendar," absolutely correct according to the exact and inspired computation preserved since the days:

Passover Dates

A.D. 29 .... Saturday, April 16
A.D. 30 .... Wednesday, April 5
A.D. 31 .... Wednesday, April 25
A.D. 32 .... Monday, April 14
A.D. 33 .... Friday, April 3

To place the Passover on a Friday in 30 A.D. is to violate one of the inspired rules of the calendar — that no common year of the sacred calendar may have 356 days. Common years of twelve months may be only 353, 354 or 355 days long — a fact that you can check in the Jewish Encyclopedia.

Some Theologians place the Passover of 30 A.D. on Friday, April 7 — 356 days after the Passover of 29 A.D. This date is two days late. The Passover in 30 A.D. was only 354 days after that of 29 A.D.

These scholars forget that God had His sacred calendar, together with the Bible, preserved since the days of Moses to this very day — and that every date of the Passover may be infallibly determined!

Moreover, astronomers recognize that the 14th of the month Nisan could have occurred on Wednesday in 30 A.D., as well as in 31 A.D. Nevertheless, if you want to believe that the crucifixion was in 30 A.D. — which it was NOT — you would still have to admit that Friday is NOT the day of the crucifixion!

For the year 31 A.D. several references, unacquainted with God's calendar, mistakenly give the Passover, Nisan 14, as Monday, March 26. But this is one month too early. The year 30 — 31 A.D. was intercalary — that is, it had 13 months — thus placing the Passover thirty days later in 31 A.D., and on a Wednesday.

During the time of Christ and up to 142 A.D., according to the rules of the Sacred Calendar, the Passover could not occur earlier than six days after the vernal equinox, which in that year occurred on March 23, about 3 a.m. Greenwich time.

Remember, in Jesus' days the equinox did not occur on March 21, but on March 22 or 23, because the Roman world was using the Julian calendar.

March 26 was only three days after the equinox; it could not have been the Passover. Therefore, in 31 A.D. the Passover was 30 days later on a Wednesday."[16]

---

[16] *http://www.hwalibrary.com/cgi-bin/get/hwa.cgi?action=getbklet&InfoID=1327166100#.VRww1UZk5CQ*

CHAPTER 11

THE WEEK THAT CHANGED THE WORLD

A. BEFORE THE FOUNDATION OF THE WORLD

God is both profound and simple when dealing with the hearts of man. Those who have encountered His presence understand the phrase *"knowing without learning"*. It describes an encounter with The Truth that awakens our spirit to the spiritual dimension we experienced while were still inside The Father. Some may call this *"knowing"* intuition or *"déjà vu."*

> *Just as He chose us in Him before the foundation of the world, that we should be holy and without blame before Him in love,*
>
> *Ephesians 1:4*

Jesus offered Himself before the foundation of the world. The week Jesus was murdered is personal for me. Although, I was not there in my physical body, my spirit was marked dramatically because of the impact it made on The Father.

In other words, the abject horror the Father felt during His Son's darkest hour was horrendous. Think about it! God was forced to turn His back during the time His Son needed Him the most.

In my opinion, that event marked the spirit of everyone who would ever become flesh. Nevertheless, before our birth each spirit made a choice that would either keep their name in the Book or remove it.

> *The beast that you saw was, and is not; and is about to come up out of the abyss and to go into destruction.* ***Those who dwell on the earth and whose names have not been written in the book of life from the foundation of the world will marvel when they see that the beast was, and is not, and shall be present.***
>
> *Revelation 17:8 WEB*

It is crucial to understand that this drama we call life, was fulfilled the same time Jesus agreed to become our sacrifice, which was before the world began. The life we are living today is the result of the choices we made then. Those of us who are serving The Father are part of His plan to awaken those, whose names are still written in The Book of Life.

Maybe this is new to you but I am fulfilling my assignment and if you are reading this book perhaps this is something The Father wants you to meditate on.

These are the types of encounters that drives me to know as much as possible, about what He did and why. I refuse to depend on another person's opinion or tradition for the event that marked my life and mankind's history forever.

There are countless books and articles written on the subject of Christ's crucifixion. My greatest guide has been The Holy Spirit, whose quickening I have grown to trust in all matters as it pertains to Christ. The tools to discover the truth are always available to those who diligently seek Him.

Nothing demonstrated the superiority of Jehovah God over the Egyptian god's more than the exodus, which delivered Israel from the iron hand of Pharaoh. That event was called *The Passover* and it is the greatest feast the Israelites were instructed to observe because it removed them out of bondage.

Following God's instructions to the letter meant the difference between life and death both physically and spiritually for the Children of Israel. Nevertheless, the Passover Feast, just as the other six feasts were only a shadow of the Messiah prophesied to come.

The Passover Lamb was the foreshadowing of their Messiah, our Lord. Moreover, it would be God's greatest coup to destroy satan and reconcile mankind.

The reason this event has been so perverted and corrupted is because God achieved everything He said He would do in the Garden of Eden.

The devil knew he could not stop God. Therefore, his only choice was to corrupt the truth, which he has done using religious witchcraft.

> *Then the LORD God said to the snake, You will be punished for this; you alone of all the animals must bear this curse: From now on you will crawl on your belly, and you will have to eat dust as long as you live.*
>
> *I will make you and the woman hate each other; her offspring and yours will always be enemies. Her offspring will crush your head, and you will bite her offspring's heel.*
>
> *Genesis 3:14-15 TEV*

The wrong interpretation surrounding this magnificent event has prevented countless millions from understanding The Christ and His finished work.

B. CHRIST FULFILLS THE LAW AS GOD'S PASSOVER LAMB

> *Do not think that I came to destroy the Law or the Prophets. I did not come to destroy but to fulfill.*
>
> *Matthew 5:17*

Then He said to them, "These are the words which I spoke to you while I was still with you, that all things must be fulfilled which were written in the Law of Moses and the Prophets and the Psalms concerning Me."

Luke 24:44

The fifteenth day of this same month is the Lord's Festival of Unleavened Bread. For seven days you must eat unleavened bread.

On the first day there will be a holy assembly. Don't do any regular work.

Leviticus 23:6-7 GW

ILLUSTRATION A:
THREE DAYS AND THREE NIGHTS

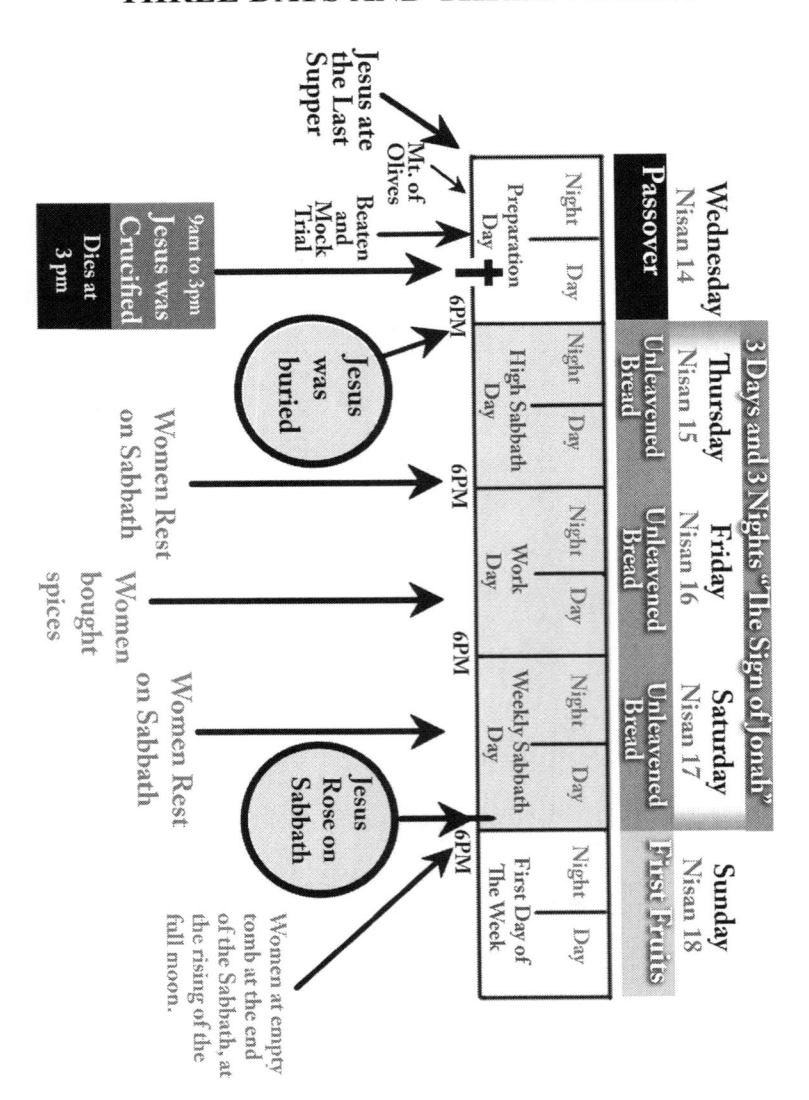

The **preparation day** was the day the Jews killed and prepared the Passover lambs during the afternoon. Those lambs were eaten after sunset.

Sunset marked the end of the "preparation day" and the beginning of the next day, a special day called the **"first day" of "Unleavened Bread"**.

We have to start with a fixed point. That fixed point is that all four Gospels clearly state that Jesus Christ was crucified and died on the preparation day, the day before the Sabbath.[17]

The following are the four passages explaining this:

> *When it was evening, there came a rich man from Arimathea, named Joseph, who himself had also become a disciple of Jesus.*
> *This man went to Pilate and asked for the body of Jesus.*
> ...
> ***Now on the next day, which is the one after the preparation****, the chief priests and the Pharisees gathered together with Pilate and said,*
> *Sir, we remember that when He was still alive that deceiver said, After three days I am to rise again.*
> Matthew 27:57-58; 62-63
>
> *'When evening had already come, **because it was the preparation day**, that is, the day before*

---

[17] *https://www.biblicalperspectives.com/books/crucifixion/2.html*

the Sabbath, Joseph of Arimathea came, a prominent member of the Council, who himself was waiting for the Kingdom of God; and he gathered up courage and went in before Pilate, and asked for the body of Jesus.

Mark 15:42-43

It was the preparation day, and the Sabbath was about to begin. *Now the women who had come with Him out of Galilee followed, and saw the tomb and how His body was laid. Then they returned and prepared spices and perfumes. And on the Sabbath they rested according to the commandment.*

Luke 23:54-56

Then the Jews, because it was the day of preparation, so that the bodies would not remain on the cross on the Sabbath (for that Sabbath was a high day), *asked Pilate that their legs might be broken, and that they might be taken away.*

John 19:31

All four gospels show that Jesus was crucified and died on the preparation day before the (HIGH DAY) Sabbath. That's the fixed point in our discussion.

The scripture in *John 19:14* does not contradict the other Gospels because during that time **Passover was considered to include all eight days of the Feast.**

The Passover always fell on the 14th day of Nisan. According to the Old Testament, Nisan is the first month of the Jewish year *(Leviticus 23:5), "In the first month, on the fourteenth day of the month at twilight is the LORD'S Passover."*

By Jewish reckoning a new day began at sundown. So at sundown, the thirteenth turned into the fourteenth day.

The Passover, better said, the first day of the Passover was also a preparation day for the High Day or annual Sabbath, which is different than the weekly Saturday Sabbath.

Passover = 8 days
Passover day + 7 days is the Feast of Unleavened Bread

The day after Passover, or the 15th day of Nisan, the seven day Feast of Unleavened bread began. The first day of the Feast of Unleavened bread was a special or (High Day) Sabbath, which prohibited any work.

> *Then on the fifteenth day of the same month there is the Feast of Unleavened Bread to the LORD; for seven days you shall eat unleavened bread.*

> *On the first day you shall have a holy convocation; you shall not do any laborious work.*

> *But for seven days you shall present an offering by fire to the LORD. On the seventh day is a holy convocation; you shall not do any laborious work.*
>
> *Leviticus 23:6-8*

Jesus was crucified on Passover, the 14th day of Nisan. But the Feast called Passover and the seven days of unleavened bread were so closely connected that they were often considered as one feast.

The Bible Knowledge Commentary New Testament, An Exposition of the Scriptures by Dallas Seminary Faculty, page 210 states:

"The one-day Passover was followed by the seven-day Feast of Unleavened Bread (Ex. 23:15; Lev. 23:4-8; Deut. 16:1-8). The entire eight-day festival was sometimes called the Passover (Luke 22:1, 7; John 19:14; Acts 12:3-4)."[18]

> *Now it was the day of preparation for the Passover; it was about the sixth hour. And he (Pilate) said to the Jews, Behold your King!*
>
> *John 19:14*

Therefore, the passage in *John 19:14*, is referring to Nisan 14 before the seven-day Feast of Unleavened Bread which began on Nisan 15, the day after Passover proper, but which was sometimes itself called the Passover week.

---

[18] *http://www.city-data.com/forum/christianity/1501796-four-gospels-agree-jesus-christ-crucified.html*

> *Now the Feast of Unleavened Bread which is called the Passover, was approaching.*
>
> ...
>
> *The day came during the Festival of Unleavened Bread when the lambs for the Passover meal were to be killed.*
>
> *Luke 22:1;7 TEV*

Remember that the seven-day Feast of Unleavened Bread began on Nisan 15, the day after Passover. Yet, as you can see in *Luke 22:1* the Feast of Unleavened Bread is called Passover as well.

That's not a contradiction or an error, it's just that in a popular sense, the entire eight day period from Nisan 14, Passover day, through the seven day Feast of Unleavened Bread ending on Nisan 21 was considered one Feast.

> *And on the first day of Unleavened Bread, when the Passover lamb was being sacrificed, His disciples said to Him, "Where do you want us to go and prepare for You to eat the Passover?"*
>
> *Mark 14:12*
>
> *Now the Feast of Unleavened Bread which is called the Passover was approaching*
>
> ...
>
> *Then came the day of unleavened bread, on which the Passover lamb had to be sacrificed.*
>
> *Luke 22:1; 7*

The understanding that Passover was always on Nisan 14, but was sometimes referred to as the first day of Unleavened Bread brings clarity to scriptures such as Mark 14:12 and Luke 22.

Jesus, knowing that He was going to be sacrificed, ate the Passover meal early on Nisan 14. Now, by Jewish reckoning, a new day began at sunset. When the sun set at 6:00 p.m. on Nisan 13 it became Nisan 14, which was Passover day.

Jesus and the disciples ate the Passover meal the evening of Nisan 14, which was according to their calendar the morning of Passover. After that meal the events that led to His crucifixion the next morning ensued. Jesus went to Gethsemane, was betrayed and arrested, and endured His trials throughout the night.
The next morning, (still Nisan 14, still Passover) Jesus was put on the cross at 9 a.m.

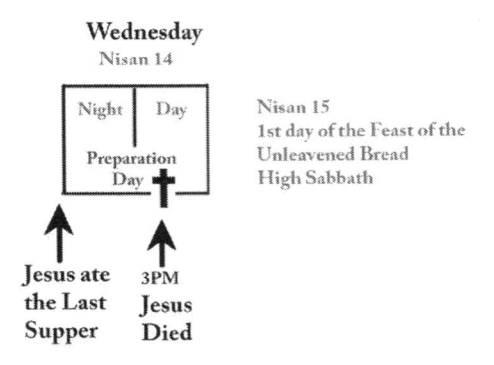

Wednesday
Nisan 14

Night	Day
	Preparation Day ✝

Nisan 15
1st day of the Feast of the Unleavened Bread
High Sabbath

↑ Jesus ate the Last Supper

↑ 3PM Jesus Died

C. SABBATHS

The Hebrew word translated "*Sabbath*" means "rest or cessation". "Sabbath" is NOT a Hebrew word for

"Saturday" or "seven." This is very important to understand.

God ordained several "Sabbaths" and also a "Special Sabbath" for Israel. These different Sabbaths were:

- The weekly 7th day Sabbath (Exodus 20:8-11)
- The Feast of Trumpets (Leviticus 23:24)
- The Day of Atonement (Leviticus 16:29)
- The 7th year Sabbath (Leviticus 25:1-4)

But the seventh day is the Sabbath of the Lord thy God.

Exodus 20:10a

Speak unto the children of Israel, saying, In the seventh month, in the first day of the month, shall ye have a Sabbath, a memorial of blowing of trumpets, an holy convocation,

Leviticus 23:24

And this shall be a statute forever unto you: that in the seventh month, on the tenth day of the month, ye shall afflict your souls, and do no work at all...

Leviticus 16:29a

But in the seventh year shall be a Sabbath of rest unto the land, a Sabbath for the Lord: thou shalt neither sow thy field, nor prune thy vineyard.

Leviticus 25:4

D. THE HIGH SABBATH

During the time while the Jews were preparing for the Passover before Jesus was crucified, John writes about this "Special Sabbath":

> *The Jews therefore, because it was the preparation that the bodies should not remain upon the cross on the Sabbath day, (for that sabbath day was an high day,)*
>
> *John 19:31a*

This High Sabbath was to start on the 15th day of Nisan when the Feast of the unleavened bread begins. The first day of that feast was a holy convocation, a day when no customary work could be done — in other words, a special Sabbath.

> *And on the fifteenth day of the same month (Nisan) is the Feast of Unleavened Bread to the Lord; seven days you must eat unleavened bread. On the first day you shall have a holy convocation; you shall do no customary work on it.*
>
> *Leviticus 23:6-7*

Jesus, being the spotless Lamb, was crucified on Passover day, Nisan 14th, and as we read in *John 19:31*, the next day (Nisan 15th) was a special Sabbath.

Per the Bible, the first day of the Feast of Unleavened Bread is a High Sabbath NO MATTER WHICH day of the week it falls on.[19]

---

[19] *http://www.6000years.org/good_wednesday.html*

We can see in the following four translations of *John 19:31* that Jesus was killed Nisan 14 or the day of Passover. Most people have been confused, thinking that because a Sabbath was about to start, it was a Saturday; But it was actually this "High Sabbath," of Nisan 15th.

It was the day of preparation, and the Jewish leaders didn't want the bodies hanging there the next day, which was the Sabbath (and a very special Sabbath, because it was the Passover). So they asked Pilate to hasten their deaths by ordering that their legs be broken. Then their bodies could be taken down.

John 19:31 NLT

Meanwhile the Jews, because it was the day of Preparation for the Passover, and in order that the bodies might not remain on the crosses during the Sabbath (for that Sabbath was one of special solemnity), requested Pilate to have the legs of the dying men broken, and the bodies removed.

John 19:31 WEY

Therefore, because it was the Preparation Day, that the bodies should not remain on the cross on the Sabbath (for that Sabbath was a high day), the Jews asked Pilate that their legs might be broken, and that they might be taken away.

John 19:31

> *Then, because it was the day of preparation, so that the bodies should not stay on the crosses on the Sabbath (for that Sabbath was an especially important one), the Jewish leaders asked Pilate to have the victims' legs broken and the bodies taken down.*
> *John 19:31 NET*

The following is the detailed description of
"Illustration A - Three Days and Three Nights"
found on Page 104.

THREE DAYS AND THREE NIGHTS

A. WEDNESDAY NISAN 14

Christ's crucifixion took place on Passover day, the 14th of Nisan, the first month in God's Sacred Calendar. This occurred in the year A.D. 31, in which Passover fell on a Wednesday.

There has been confusion because we think the Passover was the meal Jesus had with His disciples in the upper room. But Passover preceded the first day of the 7 day-feast of Unleavened Bread.

We must understand Jesus didn't eat a Passover meal; this was His last supper. Jesus, the perfect Lamb of God, was killed on Passover Day. His final meal sometimes referred to as Passover or Last supper took place Tuesday afternoon before the beginning of Wednesday, Nisan 14th on the Jewish calendar.

More confirmation is found in the book of Daniel concerning the middle of the week and that being Wednesday or Nisan 14, 31 AD.

> *And one week shall establish the covenant with many: and **in the midst of the week my sacrifice and drink-offering shall be taken away**: and on the temple shall be the abomination of desolations; and at the end of time an end shall be put to the desolation."*
>
> Daniel 9:27

Wednesday falls in the middle of the week — the very day upon which Passover fell in A.D. 31. According to the Roman calendar, this date was Wednesday, April 25.

> *"But the Jews (Judeans), because it was the day of preparation (evening of the Sabbath), they were saying, "These bodies should not pass the night on their crosses, because the Sabbath say is approaching, for that Sabbath was a high day (an annual Sabbath)." And they asked Pilate to break the legs of those who had been crucified, and they would be taken away (die quickly).*
>
> John 19:31

The time and day Jesus was crucified is recorded in *Luke 23:44-46*. Between the ninth and twelfth hour translates into between 3:00 and 6:00 p.m. our time. This is important because Thursday began at sundown, which was called The Feast of Unleavened Bread, the annual Sabbath.

Joseph of Arimathaea procured the body, wrapped it in linen (*John 19:40*) and placed it in the sepulcher (*Luke 23:50-53*). Thus, the burial took place on Passover, shortly before sunset.

B. THURSDAY NISAN 15

This is the Sabbath that is misunderstood or hidden from those who love Jesus and want to celebrate His resurrection. This book is written for you. If you understand Jesus as your Passover Lamb and His commitment to fulfill the Law it will make perfect sense.

> *Now on the next day, which was the day after the Preparation Day, the chief priests and the Pharisees were gathered together to Pilate, saying, Sir, we remember what that deceiver said while he was still alive: After three days I will rise again.*
>
> *Command therefore that the tomb be made secure until the third day, lest perhaps his disciples come at night and steal him away, and tell the people, He is risen from the dead;' and the last deception will be worse than the first.*
>
> *Pilate said to them, You have a guard. Go, make it as secure as you can.*
>
> *So they went with the guard and made the tomb secure, sealing the stone."*
>
> *Matthew 27:62-66*

The Book of Mark describes both Sabbaths.

> *And when the Sabbath was past, Mary Magdalene, and Mary the mother of James, and Salome, had bought sweet spices, that they might come and anoint Him."*
>
> Mark 16:1

Verse 2 speaks about the weekly Sabbath by saying,

> *"Very early in the morning, on the first day of the week, they came to the tomb when the sun had risen."*
>
> Mark 16:2

The phrase, *"and when the Sabbath was past"* refers to the "high day" that occurred on Thursday. Friday was the only time the women could have bought spices, since they could not do it on the weekly Sabbath, which was Saturday.

Now look at the account in Luke. These verses confirm TWO SEPARATE visits to the tomb by the women.

> *"The women who had come with Him from Galilee followed along and observed the tomb and how His body was placed.*
>
> *Then they returned and prepared spices and perfumes. **And they rested on the Sabbath according to the commandment.**"*
>
> Luke 23:55-56

Mark clearly states that the women bought the spices after the Sabbath, (High Sabbath) which fell on a Thursday during that time. Then Luke explains that the women prepared the spices and fragrant oils, after which *"they rested on the Sabbath (Saturday) according to the commandment."*

The problem is resolved if you understand that they bought the spices on Friday after they rested on the High Sabbath. Then they prepared the spices, on the same day they bought them, before resting on the weekly Sabbath or Saturday.

By comparing details in both accounts, we can clearly see that two different Sabbaths are mentioned along with a workday in between.

The first Sabbath was the annual "high day", the second was the weekly seventh-day Sabbath.

In the original Greek *Matthew 28:1* writes that the women went to the tomb *"after the Sabbath"* the word Sabbath here is actually plural and should be translated "Sabbaths."[20]

Moreover, Bible versions such as Alfred Marshall's Interlinear Greek-English New Testament, Green's Literal Translation, Young's Literal Translation and Ferrar Fenton's Translation support the "more than one Sabbath" that week.

---

[20] *http://www.scripture4all.org/OnlineInterlinear/NTpdf/mat28.pdf sabbatwn sabbatOn G4521 n_ Gen Pl n OF-SABBATHS*

And on the eve of the sabbaths, at the dawn, toward the first of the sabbaths, came Mary the Magdalene, and the other Mary, to see the sepulchre,

Matthew 28:1 YLT

C. JESUS IS THE SABBATH

In the beginning God created all things during six days but on the seventh day He rested. The Bible separates each of the six days with the phrase: *"And the evening and the morning were the... day."* This phrase is not found when describing the seventh day because this day has no beginning or ending. It is eternal because God rested "in" that day:

"Then God blessed the seventh day and set it apart as holy, because on that day he stopped all his work of creation."

Genesis 2:3 GW

Jesus is The Holy Day set apart for both God and all those who find their rest in Christ. God finished His work through Adam who was the shadow of the Last Adam.

"For in six days the LORD made the heavens and the earth, the sea, and all that is in them, and rested the seventh day. Therefore the LORD blessed the Sabbath day and hallowed it."

Exodus 20:11

"Six days shall work be done, but the seventh day is a Sabbath of solemn rest, a holy convocation. You shall do no work on it; it is the Sabbath of the LORD in all your dwellings.
Leviticus 23:3

The Laws God gave Moses were the shadow of Christ but the foundation of those laws depended on His people entering His Rest, signified as the Sabbath Day. This can only be achieved by recognizing The Christ and His finished work.

Here is another fascinating truth that will thrill you:

- Moses led the Israelites through the Red Sea the third day after leaving Egypt. That marked the end of Pharaoh and the freedom from slavery.

- Jesus resurrected on the third day, which destroyed satan and delivered mankind from slavery. Both events occurred on Nisan 17. Can you see the perfect design of God?

The resurrection of Christ on God's Sabbath is the Victory over all your enemies. But in order to experience that peace we must enter Christ as the resurrected Son. Jesus was made the Christ through His obedience and sacrifice. He is the Sabbath that we must enter. That is the description of the rebirth described to Nicodemus in *John 3*.

The writer of Hebrews makes it clear that the people of Joshua's time were looking for another "day" because there is no rest outside Christ as The Sabbath.

> *"For we who have believed do enter that rest, as He has said: 'So I swore in My wrath,' They shall not enter My rest,' although the works were finished from the foundation of the world.*
> *For He has spoken in a certain place of the seventh day in this way: "And God rested on the seventh day from all His works;*
> *and again in this place: "They shall not enter My rest.*
> *...*
> *For if Joshua had given them rest, then He would not afterward have spoken of another day."*
>
> Hebrews 4:3-5; 8

> *"There remains therefore a rest for the people of God. For he who has entered His rest has himself also ceased from his works as God did from His. Let us therefore be diligent to enter that rest, lest anyone fall according to the same example of disobedience."*
>
> Hebrews 4:9-11

Jesus rose on *"that day"* God created for Himself and all those who would recognize His finished work. The Sabbath means rest and the number seven represents perfection. Jesus embodies both names as God's perfect rest.

The religious people during the time of Jesus hated Him because He performed miracles on their Sabbath day even though He told them that day was made for man.

In other words, God created man to discover His rest in the person of Christ, not to labor under the Law. Resurrection day is the day of victory over death and rest from the labor of the law. There can be no rest following a religion or doctrine formed outside the seventh day.

The Gospel of Matthew supplies both the time and drama around the resurrection of our Lord Jesus. There are key words and descriptions that supply all the information necessary to understand Jesus as the Sabbath rose on the Sabbath.

> *"In the end of the Sabbath, as it began to dawn toward the first day of the week, came Mary Magdalene and the other Mary to see the sepulcher. And, behold, there was a great earthquake: for the angel of the Lord descended from heaven, and came and rolled back the stone from the door, and sat upon it."*
>
> *Matthew 28:1-2*

We have to read this with the Hebrew mindset that Saturday, the weekly Sabbath ended at sundown, so the dawning of Sunday was actually the beginning of the evening and the rising of the moon.

The word translated *"began to dawn"* in *Matthew 28:1* is the Greek *epiphoskousa*, which literally means "the coming of the light." *Dr. H. A. Griesemer*, a Greek scholar, has made the following remarks concerning this word:

"The word 'dawn' is very misleading. We speak of the dawn as the opening of the day, the light that comes with the rising of the sun. We associate the dawn with the sunlight, but the Greek word here is 'epiphoskousa,' which means the shining of the sun or the moon. The Passover feast always occurred at the time of the full moon. Just as the sun was setting, the moon would be rising."

Dr. George R. Berry in his Interlinear Greek-English New Testament translates the opening part of Matthew 28:1 as follows: "Now late on the Sabbath, as it was getting dusk toward the first day of the week..." We can establish the time referred to by Matthew as around 6 p.m. or the **setting of the sun on the seventh-day Sabbath**.[21]

It is extremely important that Jesus rose on the Sabbath, before the sunset, because He is the Sabbath and the rest of all the works of God. He is definitely not the *"sun god"* of Babylon, which is where the name Sunday is derived. Moreover, Jesus not only rose on the Sabbath Day but all of the earth recorded that event by violently shaking. Matthew records two major earthquakes. The first one took place when the Lord died on the cross and the veil that separated man from God was ripped. This was the Earth's response to God's Son being murdered.

> *"Behold, the veil of the temple was torn in two from the top to the bottom. The earth quaked and the rocks were split."*
> *Matthew 27:51 WEB*

---

[21] *http://rcg.org/articles/ccwnof.html#*
© *2008, 2011 The Restored Church of God*

The second came when He resurrected. This event was marked by the physical resurrection of others and that is still taking place today. This is the eternal proof that God has restored His Kingdom on earth as it is in heaven.

> *The tombs were opened, and many bodies of the saints who had fallen asleep were raised;*
> *and coming out of the tombs after his resurrection, they entered into the holy city and appeared to many.*
>
> *Matthew 27:52-53 WEB*

From His burial on Wednesday before sunset until Saturday before 6:00 p.m. is three days and three nights exactly as Jesus prophesied.

D. ROAD TO EMMAUS

We have another confirmation of the three days and three nights, when the disciples are walking on the road to Emmaus.

> *"But we were hoping that it was He who was going to redeem Israel. Indeed, besides all this, today is the third day since these things happened."*
>
> *Luke 24:21*

Here are a couple of translations that used the word *"since"* which actually means after.

The New Berkeley Version in Modern English — *Gerrit Verkugl*:

> *"Moreover, three days have already passed, since all these events occurred."*

The Syriac New Testament translated into English from *The Peshitto Version* — *James Murdock:*

> *"...and lo, three days have passed since all these things have occurred."*

E. A SUNDAY RESURRECTION IS THE BEWITCHING

Here is the key that will change your mindset. As we have said before, most people have no idea that the Bible talks about two kinds of Sabbath days. This has fueled the belief of a Sunday resurrection, which has nothing to do with Jesus being the Lord of the Sabbath. In fact, it promotes the pagan celebration of the sun god *Nimrod*.

This belief advances the assumption that the Gospels are both the beginning of the New Testament and the new religion that worships on Sunday. This deception is the witchcraft that promotes Christianity as the "New Testament replacement" for Catholicism as the intended results of the Reformation movement in the XVI century.

ALL OF THIS IS WRONG!!!! We have all been bewitched by doctrines and interpretations that are not from The Spirit of Christ. Jesus came to fulfill the Law and reestablish God's Kingdom, which celebrates Christ as ruling and reigning NOW, not in the future.

Most people have been taught to believe a lie. If you want to live your life believing a lie it is totally up to you but the Truth is the only thing that will set you free.

> *"Don't ever think that I came to set aside Moses' Teachings or the Prophets. I didn't come to set them aside but to make them come true.*
>
> *I can guarantee this truth: Until the earth and the heavens disappear, neither a period nor a comma will disappear from the Scriptures before everything has come true."*
>
> *Matthew 5:17-18 GW*

The simple placing of a page in the Bible that reads "*New Testament*" before Matthew has blindfolded the hearts and minds of generations to the truth that Jesus completed His assignment.

This nefarious act has completely hidden Jesus, as the prophetic Word, fulfilling all that was written about Him from cover to cover in the Bible.

L. EMERSON FERRELL

ILLUSTRATION B:
THE PROPHECY FULFILLED

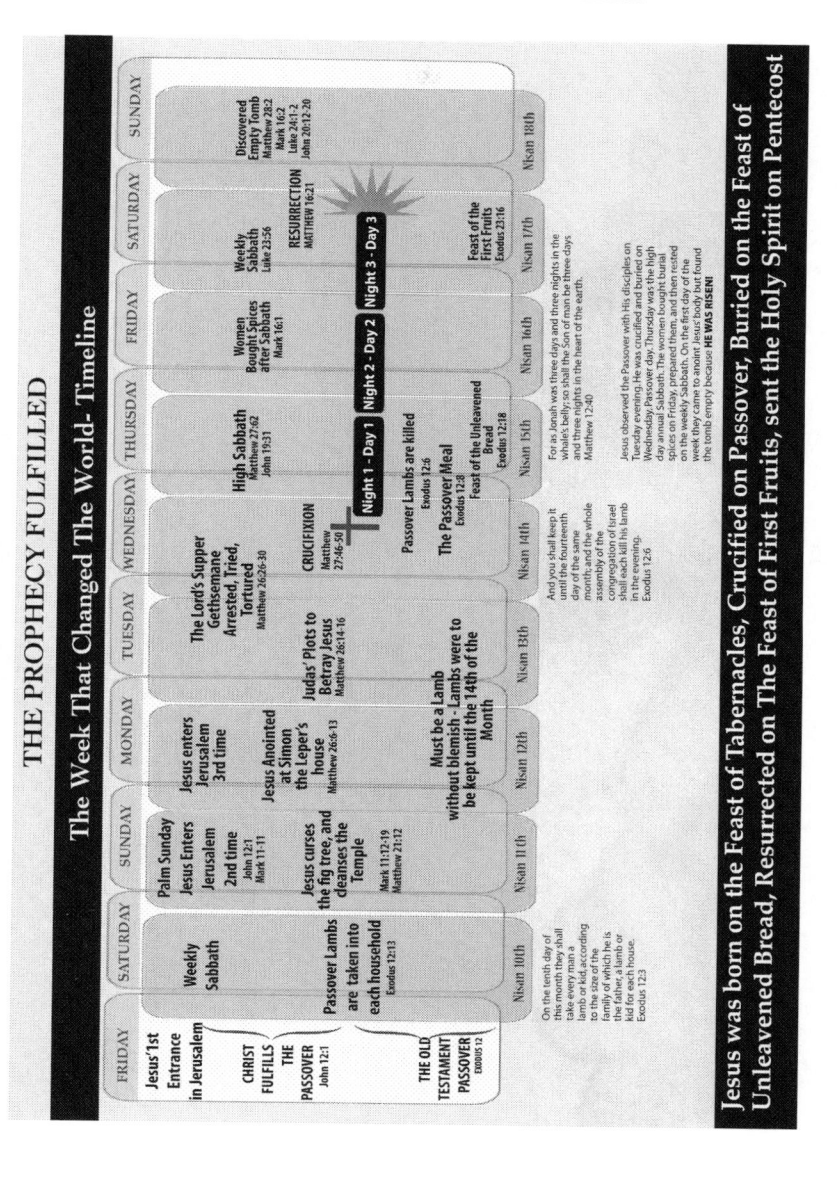

THE PROPHECY FULFILLED
The Week That Changed The World - Timeline

	FRIDAY	SATURDAY	SUNDAY	MONDAY	TUESDAY	WEDNESDAY	THURSDAY	FRIDAY	SATURDAY	SUNDAY
	Jesus' 1st Entrance in Jerusalem	Weekly Sabbath	Palm Sunday — Jesus Enters Jerusalem 2nd time — John 12:1 / Mark 11:11	Jesus enters Jerusalem 3rd time — Jesus Anointed at Simon the Leper's house — Matthew 26:6-13	The Lord's Supper Gethsemane Arrested, Tried, Tortured — Matthew 26:26-30 — Judas' Plots to Betray Jesus — Matthew 26:14-16	The Lord's Supper / CRUCIFIXION — Matthew 27:45-50	High Sabbath — Matthew 27:62 / John 19:31	Women Bought Spices after Sabbath — Mark 16:1	Weekly Sabbath — Luke 23:56 / RESURRECTION — MATTHEW 16:21	Discovered Empty Tomb — Matthew 28:2 / Mark 16:2 / Luke 24:1-2 / John 20:12-20
CHRIST FULFILLS THE PASSOVER — John 12:1		Passover Lambs are taken into each household — Exodus 12:3	Jesus curses the fig tree, and cleanses the Temple — Mark 11:12-19 / Matthew 21:12	Must be a Lamb without blemish - Lambs were to be kept until the 14th of the Month		Passover Lambs are killed — Exodus 12:6 / The Passover Meal — Exodus 12:8 / Feast of the Unleavened Bread — Exodus 12:18	Night 1 - Day 1 / Night 2 - Day 2 / Night 3 - Day 3		Feast of the First Fruits — Exodus 23:16	
THE OLD TESTAMENT PASSOVER — Exodus 12	On the tenth day of this month they shall take every man a lamb or kid, according to the size of the family of which he is the father, a lamb or kid for each house. Exodus 12:3				And you shall keep it until the fourteenth day of the same month; and the whole congregation of Israel shall each kill his lamb in the evening. Exodus 12:6		For as Jonah was three days and three nights in the whale's belly; so shall the Son of man be three days and three nights in the heart of the earth. Matthew 12:40	Jesus observed the Passover with His disciples on Tuesday evening. He was crucified and buried on Wednesday Passover day. Thursday was the high day annual Sabbath. The women bought burial spices on Friday, prepared them, and then rested on the weekly Sabbath. On the first day of the week they came to anoint Jesus' body but found the tomb empty because HE WAS RISEN!		
	Nisan 10th	Nisan 11th	Nisan 12th	Nisan 13th	Nisan 14th	Nisan 15th	Nisan 16th	Nisan 17th	Nisan 18th	

Jesus was born on the Feast of Tabernacles, Crucified on Passover, Buried on the Feast of Unleavened Bread, Resurrected on The Feast of First Fruits, sent the Holy Spirit on Pentecost

Chapter 12

THE WEEK THAT FULFILLED THE LAW

This section is to further help the reader see the Gospels as fulfilling God's Law. Each day He walked the earth it was in preparation to complete His assignment as the perfect Lamb of God. He did not come to start a new religion or to perpetuate the Law revealed to Moses.

Jesus finished the work He was assigned, in order to destroy satan and reinstate man with His Father. The last week He walked the earth, as Jesus of Nazareth, was the most important event on earth.

The books of Matthew, Mark, Luke and John are the physical record of Jesus completing His assignment and establishing God's Kingdom on earth. The profound way He achieved this is the foundational key for your prophetic walk with Christ.

You will discover that Jesus cleansed the temple each of the three times He entered Jerusalem before His final supper, arrest, trial and crucifixion. Moreover, He was anointed three times during His ministry. Do you see the importance of that number in God's redemption plan for mankind?

Nevertheless, the last two anointing's were performed by Mary of Bethany and Mary Magdalene on Nisan 10 and Nisan 12 respectively.

The graphic *(preceding this chapter)* will highlight the difference between our day and the day celebrated by the Jews that began and ended at 6 p.m. For example, Jesus celebrated the weekly Sabbath, Nisan 10 in Bethany with Lazarus, Mary and Martha before His triumphant Palm Sunday entry written about in *Matthew 21, Mark 11* and *John 12*. This was the day He cursed the Fig Tree and the following day on His last trip to Jerusalem Peter remarked that it had withered.

All of these events leading to His Last Supper, arrest, torture, crucifixion, burial and resurrection as our Sabbath are vital to study, in order for our relationship with the living Christ to "ever ascend."

The following is the detailed description of
"Illustration B - The Prophecy fulfilled"
found on Page 127.

FRIDAY
NISAN 9TH

JESUS ENTERS JERUSALEM FROM JERICHO AND CLEANSED THE TEMPLE

Luke 19:5	stays with Zacchaeus
Matthew 20:29	As they went out from Jericho, a great multitude followed him.
Matthew 21:12	Entering the Temple, Jesus drove out all who were buying and selling there, and overturned the money-changers' tables and the seats of the pigeon-dealers.
John 12:1	"Then Jesus six days before the Passover came to Bethany..."

SATURDAY
NISAN 10TH

JESUS STAYS WITH MARY, MARTHA AND LAZARUS ON THE SABBATH IN BETHANY EATS THE FIRST OF THREE MEALS MARY ANOINTED HIS FEET WITH OIL

John 12:9-12	Now it became widely known among the Jews that Jesus was there; but they came not only on His account, but also in order to see Lazarus whom He had brought back to life. The High Priests, however, consulted together to put Lazarus also to death, for because of him many of the Jews left them and became believers in Jesus.

John 12:3-7	Mary took a bottle of very expensive perfume made from pure nard and poured it on Jesus' feet. Then she dried his feet with her hair. The fragrance of the perfume filled the house.

SUNDAY
NISAN 11ᵀᴴ

THE TRIUMPHAL ENTRY
"PALM SUNDAY"
CURSING OF THE FIG TREE
CLEANSING OF THE TEMPLE

Matthew 21:1-11
Luke 19: 29-40

John 12:12,13	"On the next day much people that were come to the feast, when they heard that Jesus was coming to Jerusalem, Took branches of palm trees, and went forth to meet him, and cried, Hosanna..."
Mark 11:11	"And Jesus entered into Jerusalem, and into the temple: and when he had looked round about upon all things, and now the eventide was come, he went out unto Bethany with the twelve."
Mark 11:12-13	"And on the morrow, when they were come from Bethany, he was hungry: And seeing a fig tree afar off having leaves, he came..."

Mark 11:15   "And they come to Jerusalem: and Jesus went into the temple, and began to cast out them that sold and bought in the temple..."

Mark 11:19   "And when even was come, he went out of the city."

MONDAY
NISAN 12TH

JESUS ANOINTED THEN GOES INTO JERUSALEM THE THIRD AND LAST TIME FIG TREE WITHERED CAST OUT MONEY CHANGERS

Matthew 26:2   "Ye know that after two days is the feast of the Passover..."

Mark 14:3-10   Jesus anointed at Simon's, announces the Passover would be after two days:

Matthew 26:6-13   Jesus anointed and Judas plots to betray Him

Matthew 26:14   Then one of the twelve, who was called Judas Iscariot, went to the chief priests,

Mark 11:20   In the early morning, as they passed by, they saw the fig-tree withered to the roots;

Mark 11:21	Peter, recollecting, said to Him, "Look, Rabbi, the fig-tree which you cursed is withered up."
Luke 19:41	Weeps over the city ("they did not know their time of visitation")
Luke 19:45	He entered into the temple, and began to drive out those who bought and sold in it,

TUESDAY
NISAN 13TH

BREAD AND WINE INSTEAD OF LAMB
JESUS BETRAYED DURING THE LAST SUPPER
FOOT WASHING,
GOES TO GETHSEMANE,
AGONY IN GARDEN,
JESUS ARRESTED, TRIED
AND TORTURED THROUGH THE NIGHT.

For further study examine the scriptures below that describe the various events that occurred that evening and day:

Matthew 26:17-69
Matthew 27:1-31

Mark 14:12-53
Mark 14:1-19

Luke 22:1-54
Luke 23:1-25

John 13:1-38
John 18:1-40
John 19:1-13

WEDNESDAY
NISAN 14TH

GOD'S PASSOVER OR "PREPARATION DAY" JESUS CRUCIFIED AT 9:00 AM BURIED BY 6:00 PM IN TOMB OF JOSEPH OF ARIMATHEA

For further study examine the scriptures below that describe the various events that occurred that evening and day:

John 19:14-42
Luke 23:25-56
Mark 15:20-47
Matthew 27:26-66

THURSDAY
NISAN 15TH

HIGH SABBATH CELEBRATED FIRST DAY OF THE FEAST OF UNLEAVENED BREAD

John 19:31	"...For that Sabbath day was an high day..."
Matthew 27:62	"Now the next day, that followed the day of the preparation the chief priests and Pharisees came together unto Pilate." And secured a watch for the tomb."
Leviticus 23:6	"And on the fifteenth day of the same month is the feast of unleavened bread unto the LORD..."
Leviticus 23:7	"...Ye shall do no servile work therein." Passover Sabbath ("The Day of Passover and Unleavened Bread") Jesus in the tomb.

FRIDAY
NISAN 16TH

FIRST DAY THE WOMEN COULD PURCHASE AND PREPARE SPICES TO ANOINT HIS BODY

Mark 16:1	"And when the Sabbath was past, Mary Magdalene, and Mary the mother of James, and Salome, had bought sweet spices, that they might come and anoint him."
Luke 23:56	"And they returned, and prepared spices and ointments..."

SATURDAY
NISAN 17ᵀᴴ

WEEKLY SABBATH THE "LAST DAY" JESUS WOULD BE IN THE EARTH, THE "LAST DAY" HE SO OFTEN REFERRED TO

Luke 23:56   "And rested the sabbath day according to the commandment."

Matthew 16:21
Mark 8:3
Mark 10:34
Luke 24:7

John 11:24   Martha said to him, "I know that he will rise again in the resurrection at the last day."

JESUS THE SABBATH

RESURRECTED BEFORE 6 P.M.

3 DAYS AND 3 NIGHTS FULFILLED

SUNDAY
NISAN 18™

JESUS WAS THE FIRST FRUIT AND WAVE OFFERING, THE WOMEN WERE TOO LATE TO ANOINT HIS BODY

Lev. 23:10-11 "...Then ye shall bring a sheaf of the firstfruits of your harvest unto the priest...On the morrow after the sabbath the priest shall wave it."

Luke 24:1 "Now upon the first day of the week, very early on the morning, they came unto the sepulchre, bringing the spices which they had prepared, and certain others with them."

Mark 16:2
Matt. 28:2
Luke 24:2-3
John 20:12-19

Chapter 13

Wave Offering

Right after God gave Moses the instructions for Passover he also told him about the First Fruits/Wave Sheaf Offering:

> *"When you enter the land I am going to give you and you reap its harvest, bring to the priest a sheaf of the first grain you harvest. He is to wave the sheaf before the Lord so it will be accepted on your behalf; the priest is to wave it on the day after the Sabbath."*
>
> Leviticus 23:10-11

The Israelites were to reap the first of their harvest after the Sabbath. They could not start counting on the day of the Sabbath but had to wait till the next day. If there happened to be back to back Sabbaths that week, then they would have to wait till after the second Sabbath because they could not work (harvest) on either Sabbath.

This day is very important because the Israelites were to start counting on this day:

> *"From the day after the Sabbath, the day you brought the sheaf of the wave offering, count off seven full weeks. Count off fifty days up to the day after the seventh Sabbath and then present an offering of new grain to the Lord.*
>
> *"The priest is to wave the two lambs before the Lord as a wave offering, together with the bread of the first fruits. They are a sacred offering to the Lord for the priest."*
>
> *"On that same day you are to proclaim a sacred assembly and do no regular work. This is to be a lasting ordinance for all generations to come, wherever you live."*
>
> *Leviticus 23:13-21*
>
> *But Christ has indeed been raised from the dead, the first fruits from the dead, the first fruits of those who have fallen asleep"*
>
> *1 Corinthians 15:20*

Therefore, Jesus arose on Nisan 17, on a Saturday. He fulfilled the offering of the first of the harvest as He was the "First Fruits," and He also fulfilled the day of Pentecost by giving the Holy Spirit to all believers.[22]

---

[22] *http://www.loriswebs.com/lorispoetry/crucifix.html*

In addition, He told Mary not to touch Him because He was presenting Himself as the HOLY WAVE OFFERING for all mankind. Once The Father accepted His offering all men would have access to Him and His perfect sacrifice.

> *"Do not cling to me," said Jesus, "for I have not yet ascended to the Father. But take this message to my brethren: I am ascending to my Father and your Father, to my God and your God."*
>
> *John 20:17 WEY*

CONCLUSION

Nothing compares to the first time I met Christ Jesus. The experience is as real today as it was when I watched Billy Graham as a boy. Nevertheless, what makes that encounter so vital and rich is my never-ending pursuit to understand His ways.

> *So now — if I have, pray, found favor in your eyes, pray let me know your ways that I may (truly) know you, in order that I may find favor in your eyes:*
>
> *Exodus 33:13 Shocken Bible*

This conversation between God and Moses illustrates my overwhelming desire to understand the heart of the Father. There can be no knowledge more important between people who love one another than to understand what makes them do, what they do.

The marriage between a husband and wife in most cases begin in passion, but the ones that survive the tests of time, mature into becoming one with each other.

This maturity is formed from the decision both parties make to forget about the past and uncover the spirit of his or her mate.

It is the spirit of each person that contains the heart and soul of our Father. The passion of the physical passes, but the heart of creation is the love of our Father. God remarried His creation through the passion of Christ on the cross. The unbelievable pain and suffering Jesus bore in His body in order to save us is beyond words.

Nevertheless, He willingly laid down His life to protect His Father from any future separation that could ever be done by angels or man. The masterpiece of God's dramatic rescue and victory of mankind is both prophetically and physically implemented throughout the scriptures.

If we don't take the time to understand the way God orchestrated His greatest love gift for all humanity then we are not flesh of His flesh and bone of His bone. Jesus told the religious leaders that the sign of Jonah was the only one He would provide that verified His deity.

The Jewish leaders all knew the prophet Jonah was in the belly of the fish three days and three nights. But the churches today that after hearing the truth, still choose to preserve their pagan tradition of Good Friday and Easter Sunday will call Jesus a liar, and will follow the same spirit that crucified Him.

The power of what Jesus did is the beginning of wisdom to unlock all of the prophetic scriptures in the Bible. The next volume in this series is entitled *Before the Foundation of The World* and it will expose you to the truth of the scriptures in Daniel. The angel Gabriel was sent to warn Israel of their impending destruction but gave them 490 years to repent.

The prophetic word comes to pass but it is always given in the hopes the hearts of the people will change. This is why God is always looking for a people who will hear and change. He is never surprised by what mankind does but He always has a remnant that overcomes.

This book, and in fact the entire Resurrection Series is written for the generations that will follow, whose heart and soul are determined to know God and His ways.

I want to encourage those on the journey to *"know Him and His ways"* to never stop. The joy one finds in discovering the heart of The Father opens the door to the next dimension of Love that is reserved for His Sons.

This is the place where the secrets of the universe are shared along with the knowledge of stewardship for the riches. In future books, God willing, I will share visions and dreams that may help future generations with their assignments for restoring stewardship on this planet.

The most important event that makes all this possible is what Jesus did 2000 (+) years ago. <u>If you want to honor The Father today become familiar with the way He fulfilled His promise to you then.</u>

If you enjoyed reading this book, we also recommend

The Last Adam

Immersed in Him

The Breath of God Over Essential Oils

Quantum Fasting

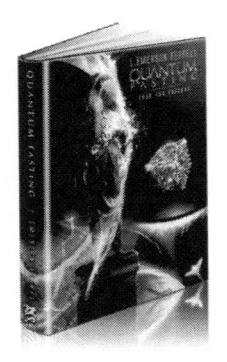

www.voiceofthelight.com

Participate in our
On Demand Courses

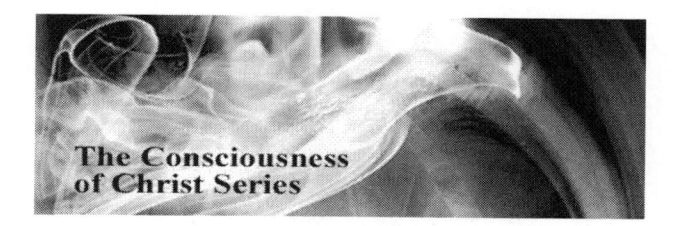

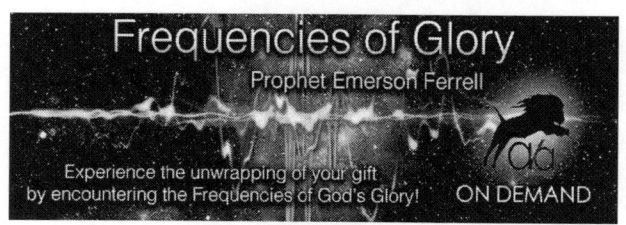

The Consciousness of Christ Series

Quantum Living
Enter the Realms of Divine Health and of a Supernatural Mind
by Emerson Ferrell

Frequencies of Glory
Prophet Emerson Ferrell
Experience the unwrapping of your gift by encountering the Frequencies of God's Glory!
ON DEMAND

EVER ASCENDING SERIES
EMERSON FERRELL
Discover your destiny IN CHRIST before the foundation of the world
ON DEMAND

on.votlm.com

Voice Of The Light Ministries

www.voiceofthelight.com

904-834-2447

P.O. Box 3418

Ponte Vedra, FL 32004

USA

Printed in Great Britain
by Amazon